Innovation or Elimination

Innovation or Elimination

Winning in a World of Constant Change

Itai Green

Innovation or Elimination: Winning in a World of Constant Change

Cover design by Cassandra Kronstedt

Interior design by S4Carlisle Publishing Services, Chennai, India

First published in 2026 by
Business Expert Press, LLC
222 East 46th Street, New York, NY 10017
www.businessexpertpress.com

ISBN-13: 978-1-60649-496-7 (paperback)
ISBN-13: 978-1-60649-497-4 (e-book)

Collaborative Intelligence Collection

First edition: 2026

10 9 8 7 6 5 4 3 2 1

EU SAFETY REPRESENTATIVE
Mare Nostrum Group B.V.
Doelen 72
4831 GR Breda
The Netherlands
gpsr@mare-nostrum.co.uk

Description

***Innovation or Elimination* is a practical manifesto for organizations determined to thrive in an era of accelerating change.**

In today's hyperconnected world, innovation is no longer optional; it's a matter of survival. *Innovation or Elimination* reveals how organizations can move beyond outdated, closed models and embrace the power of open innovation to drive real growth.

Drawing on more than two decades of hands-on experience with global corporations, start-ups, investors, and governments, the book offers a practical roadmap for transforming ideas into impact. Through real-world case studies, from Google and Android to Unilever, Ping An, and Israel's Startup Nation, the book reveals how leading organizations harness collaboration to stay ahead of disruption, particularly during crises and revolutions.

Offering a strategic framework for innovation leaders, executives, and policymakers alike, *Innovation or Elimination* explores the cultural, structural, and leadership transformations required to embed open innovation within organizations. It concludes with actionable tools for mapping ecosystems, engaging start-ups, measuring success, and striking a balance between short-term performance and long-term vision.

In particular, this book is ideal for executives, board members, innovation leaders, entrepreneurs, controlling shareholders and policymakers who aspire to transform their organizations into more agile, future-ready enterprises but are uncertain about the most effective strategies to do so or have encountered previous failures. Regardless of experience level, *Innovation or Elimination* provides actionable insights, proven frameworks, and a fresh perspective to take innovation to the next level, drive it to successful execution as well as best practices for entrepreneurs with respect to how to best deal with corporations.

Contents

List of Figures

Review Quotes

"Itai Green's Innovation or Elimination *is not just a guide to frameworks or best practices. It is a manifesto for a new kind of leadership, one that understands that innovation no longer happens within walls but across networks. Itai reminds us that ideas need oxygen, and oxygen comes from openness: open minds, open partnerships, open ecosystems."*—**Alberto Onetti, Chairman of Mind the Bridge; Professor of Entrepreneurship, University of Insubria**

"This book stands out because it blends strategic insight with practical guidance, offering a comprehensive roadmap for organizations seeking to embrace open innovation. A unique feature of this book is its integration of emerging technologies, such as AI, generative AI, and quantum computing, into the open innovation narrative. It explains how these technologies reshape collaboration models and influence organizational structures and strategies, reinforcing the need for interconnected networks rather than siloed efforts."—**Eugene Acevedo, Author; Former President and CEO, RCBC**

"What stands out is the author's experience. This is not theory at arm's length. It is lived insight from decades spent at the intersection of technology, strategy, and enterprise. The stories, frameworks, and lessons offered here reflect real-world success and the painful consequences of failing to adapt."—**Andrew Constable, MBA, Managing Partner and Senior Strategy Consultant, Visualise Solutions**

"What struck me most as I read this book is how it reframes innovation from a competitive advantage into a collective necessity. We no longer innovate to outpace one another. Instead, we innovate to stay relevant in a world that refuses to slow down. The challenge is not in having ideas, as the streets are littered with ideas. The challenge lies in creating the conditions and a safe space where ideas can collide and evolve."—**Thomas Koulopoulos, Author of Gigatrends; Chairman, Delphi Group**

"Innovation is not a slogan or a ceremonial ribbon-cutting exercise. It is a fundamental requirement for survival in a world where the pace of change outstrips the pace at which most organizations evolve. The insights in this book are not theoretical constructs gathered from a distance but are drawn from real work across global corporations, government agencies, academic institutions, and start-up ecosystems where groundbreaking ideas are born. This book is an invitation to adopt that mindset. It is a practical guide for leaders who understand that innovation is not a side project but the operating system of modern business. Those who embrace openness will shape the future. Those who do not will be shaped by it."—**Alex Goryachev, *WSJ* Bestselling Author; Former GM of Cisco's Global Innovation Centers**

Foreword

Innovation or Elimination is not just another book on innovation. It is a call to action from Itai Green, who has lived the full spectrum of innovation practice as an innovation architect, an innovation builder, and at times, a challenger of the status quo.

As an innovator, you will deeply recognize and appreciate the central message of this work: innovation does not flourish behind closed doors. It thrives in openness and in ecosystems where ideas collide, where curiosity outpaces ego, and where diverse minds collaborate to create value that none could achieve alone. The book highlights this truth with clarity and practicality. It invites us to move beyond familiar comfort zones and into shared creation, where innovation becomes a living, evolving force rather than a slogan.

As a consultant, you will appreciate how the author avoids romanticizing innovation. Itai acknowledges the organizational realities: the bureaucracy, the fear of risk, and the weight of legacy systems. And yet, through credible examples and grounded frameworks, he shows that meaningful change is possible when leaders choose to be intentional, consistent, and courageous.

As a manager, you will be struck by the honesty of the core insight: Innovation is not optional; it is existential. In a world of accelerating technological and competitive shifts, organizations must choose to innovate or be overtaken. The title is a reality we must confront.

Innovation or Elimination offers both direction and inspiration. It bridges vision with pragmatism. It does not merely explain why we must innovate; it shows how to begin. Take this book as your invitation to lead yourself forward. The future is shaped by those who choose to.

Innovative regards,

Gijsbertus J.J. van Wulfen
Founder
FORTH Innovation Methodology

A Note from the Author

Writing this book has been one of the most meaningful journeys of my professional life. It began, like many of my projects, with a spark: I wanted to write down what I have learned through years of working with corporations, start-ups, governments, and entrepreneurs who, in their own ways, have all shaped my understanding of innovation.

This book was written during my flights to Paris, New York, Berlin, Athens, Bangkok, Madrid, Tokyo, and Santo Domingo. It was written in the quiet moments after lectures in South Korea, Portugal, Switzerland, Canada, Argentina, Israel, and Brazil, during early mornings when new ideas took form, and in late nights of reflection after meetings that challenged my previous thoughts. Each chapter was an attempt to capture lessons gathered from countless conversations, projects, successes, and failures. I hoped to distill not only methods but also the spirit of open innovation: collaboration, humility, and continuous learning.

Above all, this book could not have been written without the support of the people closest to me.

Acknowledgments

My deepest thanks go to Tagil, my wife. Your strategic mind, creative instinct, and unwavering belief in this work shaped every stage of this book. You challenged ideas, refined messages, and helped transform scattered insights into a coherent vision. Your influence is present on every page, and none of this would have been possible without you.

I extend my deep gratitude to Tal Gur-Arye, my right hand for nearly a decade. Tal's analytical thinking, academic depth, and exceptional writing abilities played a central role in the research, editing, and conceptual framework of this book, as well as in applying these same ideas in the field, working with clients worldwide, and translating theory into tangible results. Simply put, this book could not exist without Tal.

I am grateful to the many colleagues, clients, and partners across corporations, start-ups, and public institutions who have trusted me with their challenges and ambitions. Your openness, curiosity, and willingness to experiment have shaped my understanding of innovation far more than any theory. Every engagement, whether identifying needs, running pilots, implementing solutions, or debating ideas, has expanded my perspective on what truly drives meaningful change.

I owe special thanks to Amadeus, the company that first exposed me to the global world of innovation; to Gabby Czertok, whose mentorship introduced me to open innovation long before it became mainstream; and to Professor Henry Chesbrough, whose pioneering academic work continues to inspire my thinking.

To all the hundreds of organizations that have invited me to speak around the world, thank you for your challenging questions and diverse perspectives. These interactions have played a central role in refining the ideas presented in this book and in shaping my belief in innovation as a living, evolving practice.

Special appreciation goes to Yaron Flint, who encouraged me to turn this idea into a book and guided me through the earliest stages of the process.

I would also like to thank the publishing team at Business Expert Press, especially Scott Isenberg, Jim Spohrer, and Charlene Kronstedt, for their professionalism, insights, and support in shaping the manuscript into its final form.

Finally, my deepest gratitude goes to my children, Daniel, Ron, and Guy, who remind me daily why innovation matters. Your curiosity, courage, and endless questions inspire me to keep exploring, learning, and imagining a better future. Everything I do is, in some way, for you.

Thank you all for being part of this journey.

Itai Green

Introduction

Not long ago, innovation was a fortress. Companies kept their ideas under lock and key, believing that success depended on secrecy and control and could only be achieved through internal resources. For a time, this may even have been true.

That world is now long gone. Today, the most successful organizations recognize that **innovation thrives not behind closed doors but at the intersection of diverse minds, experiences, and skills**. This is the era of open innovation, the only approach that enables organizations to collaborate with the brightest minds and leverage external technologies and partnerships, thereby creating immense value through shared efforts.

Before diving into the concept of open innovation, it is important to pause and ask a more fundamental question: what is innovation, and why does it matter? At its core, innovation is the ability to turn new ideas into meaningful impact, whether through products, services, processes, or business models that create real value. It is not merely about invention or creativity; it is about successful implementation and adoption. Without embedding innovation into an organization's DNA, even the most brilliant ideas remain unrealized.

In a world defined by accelerating change, companies that fail to embrace innovation, especially open innovation, risk stagnation and eventual decline. Disruption is no longer a distant threat; it is an immediate reality. Those who cling to old models will be outpaced by more agile competitors and, ultimately, left behind.

In this environment, adopting innovation is not optional; instead, it is a matter of survival, and **open innovation is the most efficient way to innovate successfully.** That is why I am happy to share this book with you and to serve as a guide in navigating the shift from closed to open innovation.

I am proud to say this is not another theoretical guide written from the sidelines. It is built on more than two decades of real-world experience: from founding and scaling start-ups to leading innovation in major corporations, serving as a board member, and managing director; from advising CEOs and government ministers to working hands-on with accelerators, VCs, and global tech ecosystems. I have had the privilege of living and breathing innovation from every angle: private, public, academic, and entrepreneurial.

I have led hundreds of innovation workshops and keynote conferences worldwide, helping organizations connect the dots between emerging technologies and pressing business challenges. I have seen firsthand, time and time again, how open innovation can transform stagnation into growth, bureaucracy into agility, and disconnected ideas, challenges, and fears into breakthrough products and services.

In this book, you will learn how to transform innovation from a concept into a practice. You will discover how to move from "closed" to "open" innovation, and how to design, manage, and scale innovation ecosystems that connect corporations, start-ups, investors, academia, and governments. We will explore the evolution of open innovation, the key structures and cultures that support it, and the practical tools required to implement it successfully, including ecosystem mapping, risk management, and strategic alignment, as well as measuring outcomes and embedding innovation across departments.

You will also encounter real-world case studies from global leaders, such as Google, Unilever, Walmart, and Ping An, among many others, that have successfully leveraged open innovation to transform their industries. Together, we will explore how economic, technological, and geopolitical crises can serve as catalysts for innovation rather than threats, and how emerging technologies, including but not limited to artificial intelligence (AI) and generative AI are reshaping the innovation landscape.

Drawing on my experience working alongside notable partners at the intersection of technology, innovation, and enterprise, along with the global case studies and insights presented throughout, this book will serve as a practical roadmap for succeeding in a rapidly changing world.

Whether you're a corporate executive, a start-up founder, a policy maker, an academic, or an innovation consultant, this book will challenge your assumptions, spark new ideas, and most importantly, offer concrete steps toward unlocking the full potential of open innovation.

Because in our connected world, no one can truly innovate by themselves.

PART 1

The Theory

CHAPTER 1

Open Innovation in a Nutshell

The arrogance of success is to think that what you did yesterday will be sufficient for tomorrow.

—Professor William G. Pollard

In a nutshell, open innovation is not just about simply embracing external ideas. Instead, it is about creating an interconnected ecosystem where creativity, agility, and collaboration thrive, **enabling the creation of mutual value for all participants within the ecosystem**. While other methods may promise growth for organizations, none is as successful or efficient in terms of resources and time as open innovation. In this book, you will learn everything there is to know about open innovation and how to use it to ensure that your organization is ready for whatever the future may bring.

Innovation has always been a cornerstone of progress and success. Throughout history, it has driven growth, reshaped industries, and transformed societies. From the invention of the printing press to the dawn of the Internet, innovation has been pivotal in human development. It should come as no surprise, then, that some **83 percent**[1] **of respondents in a 2024 Boston Consulting Group (BCG) survey named innovation as one of the top three priorities.**

While there is an obvious growing understanding of the importance of innovation, corporate leaders, including managers, owners, and board members, who are fully honest with themselves, will admit that this goes deeper than this: something has changed.

---

[1]Boston Consulting Group, "83% of Companies Rank Innovation as a Top-Three Priority, Yet Just 3% Are Ready to Deliver on Those Innovation Goals," June 4, 2024.

The approach to innovation in successful organizations has undergone significant evolution in recent years, shifting from a model of isolated, internal research and development to one defined by collaborative ecosystems, external partnerships, and the integration of outside expertise. Understanding this shift is crucial for any organization that wants to remain competitive. Organizations must realize that there is no longer time to spare in the race for success. We are not talking about the need to change to be successful a decade from now, and not even tomorrow. **Companies must innovate to remain relevant and competitive in today's market.** When I deliver my lectures to corporations worldwide, I usually open my speech by quoting Professor William G. Pollard, the American physicist, who said that the arrogance of success is to think that what you did yesterday will be sufficient for tomorrow. Organizations that understand this and innovate through open innovation will empower themselves to adapt and thrive in this fast-changing reality. This is a lesson that organizations must quickly learn, or they will be left far behind both current and future competitors.

Open innovation, which we will explore together in this book, is a collaborative approach that involves working with external partners and sources of knowledge to maximize value creation while minimizing the resources required for innovation. Open innovation will be defined in further detail in the following chapters; however, for now, it is important to understand that leveraging external partners and knowledge is the only guarantee that an organization will not be caught off guard by innovative technology. An organization that practices innovation correctly, as described in this book, is far less likely to be caught off guard by disruption than one relying solely on a consulting firm's report, which is often limited, based on a specific moment in time, and grounded in less industry knowledge than the organization itself possesses.

Open innovation reflects the reality that no organization can single-handedly keep up with today's technological and behavioral change rate. The smartest ideas often originate from outside the boundaries of a singular company, necessitating organizations to collaborate across different limits, industries, and geographies.

This enables corporate leaders not only to be receptive to external ideas and voices but also to eliminate internal politics and excuses that often serve as barriers to change.

The following chapters will explore the origins and evolution of innovation, while presenting how innovation trends have evolved over time, and highlighting the transition from closed innovation to open innovation, allowing you, the reader, to better understand how and why this model has become indispensable for any organization striving to stay competitive and relevant.

CHAPTER 2

Why Innovation Matters in a Dynamic World

$500? Fully Subsidized? That is the most expensive phone in the world, and it doesn't appeal to business customers because it doesn't have a keyboard.

—Steve Ballmer

In today's world, **innovation is no longer a luxury**. Traditional models of growth, which relied heavily on predictable markets, long-term product cycles, and in-house research and development, are no longer sufficient to keep organizations competitive, and businesses, governments, and societies face challenges that are complex and interconnected.

The pace of technological development today is truly breathtaking. **According to Moore's law, computing power doubles approximately every two years**; however, the ramifications of technological progress extend far beyond hardware. **Consider this: it took 75 years for the telephone to reach 50 million users. The Internet? Four years. It took ChatGPT just 60 days to double this number, reaching 100 million users** (Figure 2.1).

This exponential adoption of technology is fueled by the "network effect," where the value of a specific technology increases as more people and organizations adopt it, which in turn influences the adoption decision itself.[2] In recent years, our world has evolved from six degrees of separation to what feels like a flat, boundaryless world that amplifies the speed at which innovations spread, creating unprecedented opportunities for impact and disruption.

---

[2] R. Beck, D. Beimborn, T. Weitzel, and W. König, "Network Effects as Drivers of Individual Technology Adoption: Analyzing Adoption and Diffusion of Mobile Communication Services," *Information Systems Frontiers* 10 (2008): 415–429.

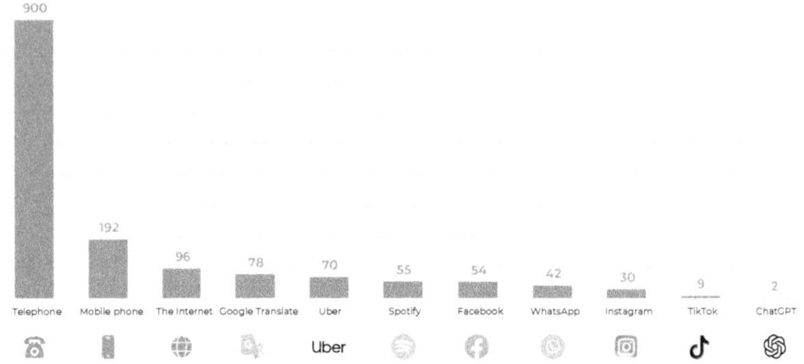

Figure 2.1 Months to reach 100 million monthly active users

Source: UBS; Boston Consulting Group; Statista; Mobile Phone History; Scientific American Internet Live Stats; VentureBeat; Wired; Digital Quarterly; TechCrunch; App.Mtr.com; OS X Daily; Fortune; Business Insider/Yahoo.

AI, robotics and process automation, the Internet of Things (IoT), Blockchain, human/machine augmentations, augmented, virtual, and synthetic realities, nanotechnology, synthetic biology, biomimicry, quantum computing, clean energy solutions and other disruptive advances are all transforming industries at a rate that outpaces our ability to predict or prepare for their impacts, or are set to do that in the near future. If you, the reader, grew up watching science fiction, you may recall how many technologies were predicted by series and films like Star Trek, going back to the 1960s. But now? **We are heading into uncharted territories.** Moreover, innovations in one sector are now often cascading into others, creating ripple effects across industries in a way that changes both businesses and behavior.

Recent data show just how rapidly this shift is unfolding. According to BCG[3] the majority of global organizations (61 percent) are already investing in AI technologies such as machine learning. Robotics and process automation follow at 46 percent, and the IoT and edge computing at 44 percent. Emerging areas such as Blockchain, Web3, and DeFi (29 percent); human/machine augmentation (29 percent); augmented, virtual, and synthetic realities (27 percent); nanotechnology and synthetic biology (16 percent); and quantum computing (10 percent) are

[3]Boston Consulting Group, "BCG Global Innovation Survey 2023," *BCG Analysis*, 2023.

also gaining meaningful attention. These figures reflect not only where companies see immediate value but where they anticipate future disruption and opportunity.

Innovations in one sector increasingly ripple through others, creating cascading effects that transform both business models and human behavior. For instance, the rise of generative AI tools, such as ChatGPT or Midjourney, a topic that will be discussed in detail later, has redefined how companies and individuals approach creativity, efficiency, accessibility, and transparency of data, as well as fundamental interactions.

Organizations leveraging these technologies can deliver personalized customer experiences, reduce costs, and create entirely new value propositions to meet customer expectations and remain relevant. For individuals, failing to adapt to innovation risks becoming less relevant in the job market, whether they are seeking their next role, aiming for a promotion, or simply trying to maintain their current position. Hence, there is an incentive for employees to actively engage with innovation, resulting in value for both the individual and the organization.

Individuals and companies that resist these shifts, as well as those who want to adapt but lack the necessary tools, are left playing catch-up. This is evident in the disruptions faced by companies like Kodak, Blockbuster, and Nokia, all classic case studies of once-market leaders who failed to adapt to the transformative forces around them.

Moreover, **innovation matters not simply because of rapid technological advancements but also due to profound societal and consumer shifts, and because organizations overwhelmingly view it as a core driver of business performance.** According to the PwC,[4] 97 percent of firms identify increased profits and sales as a key motivation for innovation, 96 percent cite improved customer satisfaction, and 94 percent highlight market expansion. Additional drivers include greater efficiency (91 percent), brand reinforcement (88 percent), attracting talent (82 percent), increasing the number of ideas (76 percent), and reducing time to market (73 percent). These data points clearly demonstrate that innovation is not an abstract ideal but a strategic necessity grounded in measurable business priorities.

---

[4]PwC, "PwC Innovation Report Survey," 2018.

For example, the aging global population puts pressure on industries such as health care and financial services, and in truth, any business based on service, to find new ways to deliver personalized and efficient solutions. Likewise, urbanization and migration patterns are transforming cities, demanding smarter infrastructure, while changing workforce expectations push organizations to adopt more flexible, inclusive, and sustainable practices. These dynamics make innovation necessary to address evolving societal needs, not simply technological ones.

Consumer expectations are another driving force. **Modern consumers demand immediacy, customization, and transparency, as well as a hyperpersonalized experience.** They expect businesses to align with their values and offer them the same level and quality of experience that they have grown to expect from technological leaders. For example, fast-fashion retailers relying on unsustainable production risk falling out of favor. It goes further, as banks, insurers, health organizations, energy companies, and manufacturers are all facing new demands and expectations, often out of their core activities and processes. This is not limited solely to consumers; employees are also interested in working in relevant organizations that keep pace with changing times. **Organizations that can anticipate and respond to these changing demands are not just more likely to succeed; they are better positioned to lead.** By understanding emerging expectations before competitors, they can set new standards, capture customer loyalty, and attract top talent seeking relevance and purpose. A proactive stance also creates a self-reinforcing cycle, where innovation draws more partners, resources, and public trust, which in turn further amplifies their competitive advantage.

Another element of how dynamic our world is today, is that in a globalized economy, **the concept of a "local" competitor has eroded**. No longer does an American company operating in a specific field compete with another American company in the same field, but **a start-up in Tel Aviv or Bangalore can develop a technology that disrupts the whole industry within months, and a Canadian or Japanese corporation in an entirely different sector can suddenly become a competitor**. For example, Alibaba transitioned into the tourism industry, utilizing robots, and in 2018, it debuted a mega vending machine, showcasing its potential in the automotive industry. Who could have foreseen such a move from the retail giant? Who would have also imagined that Amazon would become a player in the insurance and health care industries? This demonstrates that a company in Brazil, for example, which is now required to compete against large Chinese or American corporations entering its market, must remain at the forefront of innovation. **The world, therefore, has become a tightly woven fabric of both competition and collaboration, where businesses must innovate quickly and efficiently or risk becoming obsolete.**

As a result of these global macrotrends, recent research shows that innovation capabilities consistently rank among the top three sources of competitive advantage across nearly all industries. According to McKinsey,[5] the "ability to innovate" is cited as the leading factor contributing to an organization's competitive edge, far surpassing customer relationships, talent, operational excellence, commercial capabilities, corporate culture, and even global footprint. This pattern holds across various sectors, including high tech, health care, automotive and assembly, retail, energy, consumer goods, and financial services.

Innovation, particularly through disruptive technologies, is crucial for gaining a competitive edge. AI and GenAI, two significant technologies that I will discuss in further detail later, are examples of key drivers of competitive advantage, directly influencing companies' market value and financial performance.

Organizations that successfully integrate such capabilities into their core operations consistently outperform their peers, a trend strongly supported by recent financial data. According to McKinsey's[6] analysis of S&P 500 sectors, companies that lead in digital and AI capabilities significantly outperform laggards in total shareholder return across insurance, consumer industries, and energy and materials. In the insurance sector, digital and AI leaders achieved a compound annual growth rate of 6.7 percent, compared with only 1.1 percent among laggards. In consumer industries, leaders reached 9.4 percent TSR versus 3.2 percent for laggards, while in energy and materials, leaders posted 11.6 percent compared with 5.0 percent.

---

[5]McKinsey & Company, "Strategic Growth and Innovation Survey," 2024.
[6]McKinsey & Company, "The Year 2024: The Year in Charts," December 11, 2024.

These disparities highlight a clear pattern: organizations that invest in digital transformation and advanced AI capabilities gain a substantial and measurable financial advantage. The evidence indicates that the key strategic question is no longer whether companies should innovate **but how they should do it in the most efficient manner.**

Lessons Learned from Corporate Giants and Their Start-Up Collaborations: Google and Android

In 2005, Google acquired Android, a relatively unknown start-up that was working on an open-source mobile operating system. Google recognized that mobile computing would soon eclipse desktops, and therefore made a calculated bet, acquiring the company for $50 million.

Instead of fully absorbing Android into its corporate structure, Google allowed Android to retain much of its autonomy under its founder, Andy Rubin. This allowed Android to remain agile, while Google provided the necessary financial resources and market reach to scale and ultimately dominate the market.

Lessons Learned:

1. Corporations should resist the instinct to fully integrate acquired start-ups if doing so will slow down innovation.
2. Timing is critical, and Google's timely acquisition of Android came before the mobile revolution peaked, giving it a crucial first-mover advantage. Understanding where the winds were blowing at the time was key to this success.
3. Android had a strong foundation, but Google's distribution, marketing, and resources propelled it to dominance.

Internal Innovation is not enough. While internal R&D departments may have been enough to innovate in an era of slower market changes, they now struggle to keep pace with the agility required in a contemporary age, and today's innovation challenges require a diversity of perspectives, faster decision making, and access to emerging technologies.

Moreover, both the scope and severity of business challenges have expanded. Organizations must now address new challenges, including climate change, global pandemics, shifting consumer expectations, and economic volatility. **These challenges demand solutions that transcend organizational boundaries**, drawing on the collective knowledge and resources of diverse stakeholders, and the ability to provide solutions quickly like never before. As Marco Iansiti and Roy Levien[7] pointed out in 2004, the fates of organizations are intertwined, with the survival of different members of an ecosystem influenced by other members. Therefore, organizations must look beyond their own boundaries to develop holistic strategies.

For example, a single company or government cannot drive the transition to a net-zero economy. For instance, successful renewable energy solutions often depend on partnerships between tech companies developing smart grid technologies, start-ups working on energy storage innovations, and governments creating supportive policies. Similarly, industries like banking, insurance, and retail face similar challenges. Staying competitive means collaborating with tech start-ups, as well as other key ecosystem actors, to integrate solutions such as AI-powered fraud detection, personalized marketing algorithms, climate risk models, and other technological solutions that help adapt to and address new challenges.

For those who hesitate, the risks are clear: irrelevance and decline in a world that rewards adaptability and even punishes inertia. As you continue reading, keep in mind the basic promise at the heart of this book: organizations must push for **innovation, or risk elimination.**

---

[7] M. Iansiti and R. Levien, "Strategy as Ecology," *Harvard Business Review* 82, no. 3 (2004): 68–81.

CHAPTER 3

From Closed Innovation to Open Innovation

You fly to Blockbuster, try and sell the business, and they laugh at you. [...] I think the more important lesson—a lesson that Blockbuster learned too late—is simply this: "If you are unwilling to disrupt yourself, there will always be someone willing to disrupt your business for you."

—Marc Randolph

The world of innovation has undergone a dramatic transformation over the past few decades, accompanied by a conceptual reboot. In my native tongue, this is something that we would call "changing your floppy disk," which is similar to the English phrase of "flipping a switch." These only show how quickly technology advances, and even language, which is traditionally quick to adapt, is not fast enough to keep pace with the change.

The evolution of innovation practices has been marked by a significant shift from the traditional "closed innovation" model, characterized by siloed in-house research and development, to a collaborative and networked approach that can quickly create value for all ecosystem participants. Here, I will present the historical context, some key breakthroughs, and, of course, the driving forces behind this transformation in how organizations innovate.

Historically, businesses relied heavily on the closed innovation model, where research and development were conducted entirely in-house. Companies using this methodology relied on their internal resources, assuming that the necessary knowledge and capabilities resided within their walls.

Major corporations, such as Nokia, IBM, and General Electric, exemplified the closed innovation methodology, investing heavily in proprietary research to maintain competitive advantages while prioritizing tight control over intellectual property and the utilization of internal resources.

The prevailing belief that led these companies was that the best ideas and their execution could only come from within their own walls. Therefore, secrecy was viewed as essential for maintaining a competitive edge.

This model dominated the corporate landscape for much of the twentieth century, until technological changes and the growing spread of young tech start-ups made companies realize that internal innovation was not enough.

And why? Since this approach has had some significant drawbacks. While the model has proven effective in a much slower-moving world, it has faced growing limitations and challenges as industries began to evolve at an accelerating rate. In fact, as markets became increasingly complex and dynamic, companies found it challenging to keep pace with the rapid technological advancements, shifting consumer demands, and growing competition from a globalized economy.

This closed innovation model often resulted in slower innovation cycles and higher costs, and organizations that were led by this approach frequently missed out on external insights and creative ideas that could have enriched their innovation efforts. Moreover, as products themselves have become increasingly digitalized and complex in recent years, the limitations of a closed model have grown even more evident, since no single organization can master all the required technologies and disciplines internally. As a result, **closed innovation ultimately left companies outpaced, less innovative, and even replaced entirely by more agile competitors.**

Enter open innovation.

In terms of timeframe, open innovation is not a new concept. Its roots go back as far as the Longitude Act of 1714,[8] in which the British Parliament decided to provide rewards to inventors to draw upon ideas and external innovation after a particularly tragic naval disaster, when four Royal Navy warships were lost off the coast of the Isles of Scilly, and some 2,000 sailors lost their lives. The disaster had been attributed to the navigators' inability to calculate their position accurately, and the British Parliament chose to attempt to draw upon external innovation to find

[8] R. W. Spencer, "Open Innovation in the Eighteenth Century. *Research-Technology Management* 55 no. 4 (2012): 39–43.

a solution. The act clearly defined the challenge, described the desired outcome, provided clear measures for testing success, established a review team, and, of course, offered a meaningful reward.

The late twentieth century marked a much-needed turning point with the realization that something had to change, and closed innovation was just not enough. This initiated the conceptualized model of open innovation as we know it today. This approach would be later popularized in 2003 by Professor Henry Chesbrough, who first coined the term "Open Innovation" in his book "Open Innovation: The New Imperative for Creating and Profiting from Technology," challenging the traditional notion that innovation must be confined within the boundaries of a single organization.

Instead, open innovation finally recognizes that valuable ideas and technologies exist outside the company's walls and encourages partnerships with external stakeholders such as start-ups, universities, suppliers, and even competitors. By tapping into the broader ecosystem and utilizing this new methodology, organizations can access a more diverse perspective, reduce costs, and accelerate their time to market.[9]

This concept, which is now common knowledge among innovative organizations, was unprecedented at the time.

Lessons Learned from Corporate Giants and Their Start-Up Collaborations: Walmart and Plenty

Retail supply chains have relied on traditional farming and long-haul logistics to deliver fresh produce for years. In 2022, Walmart partnered with Plenty, a start-up specializing in AI-driven vertical farming, which enables year-round farming, significantly reduces water consumption, minimizes land requirements, enhances crop yields, and reduces the need for pesticides.

Walmart invested in Plenty and signed a long-term commercial agreement, integrating the start-up's produce into its distribution network.

[9] H. W. Chesbrough, *Open Innovation: The New Imperative for Creating and Profiting from Technology* (Harvard Business School, 2003).

Lessons Learned:

1. Start-ups can help corporations to futureproof their supply chains.
2. Long-term commitments create stability for start-ups. Rather than a one-time pilot, Walmart's multiyear partnership ensured Plenty had a guaranteed market for its products.
3. Corporations should be on top of trends and see them as a competitive advantage.

It was not a coincidence that open innovation emerged when it did; several key developments and macro trends have fueled its growth. Globalization has interconnected markets like never before, making it clear that no single company could monopolize knowledge or expertise. At the same time, new competition rose due to globalization, where companies could suddenly be toppled by new challengers from anywhere in the world and at any time. Similarly, advancements in digital technologies and the Internet revolutionized communication, enabling seamless collaboration across geographic boundaries.

The emergence of technology and innovation hubs, including Silicon Valley, New York, Tel Aviv, and London, introduced a new culture of risk-taking and partnerships, further demonstrating the power of external collaboration. In the early days of this shift, collaboration between academia, start-ups, and corporations laid the groundwork for open innovation. For example, the partnership between universities and early Silicon Valley tech firms helped foster breakthrough research and innovations. Netscape, the first graphical web browser, is an example of the impact that Silicon Valley had on the commercialization of the Internet. Similarly, the early alliances between Intel and IBM in the 1980s enabled the rapid development of microprocessor-based computing.

Lastly, shifting consumer preferences and market dynamics demanded, then as they still do now, greater agility, which open innovation networks were uniquely positioned to provide, further fueling the rise of this innovation methodology.

Several pivotal moments defined the transition from closed, internal innovation to open innovation. For example, the advent of crowdsourcing platforms allowed organizations to tap into the collective wisdom of a global audience, democratizing the innovation process. Open-source movements, particularly in the software industry, have proven that collaborative development can produce superior products while reducing costs. Corporate innovation labs became critical tools for scouting external ideas, piloting emerging technologies, and forging strategic partnerships with start-ups. Moreover, ecosystems where multiple stakeholders, such as universities, research institutions, start-ups, and corporations, have come together to share risks and rewards showcase the potential of collaborative innovation on a larger scale.

The growing popularity of the Internet in the 1990s is another contributing factor that has made it easier for companies to collaborate with external partners regardless of geographic location. This facilitated the exchange of ideas and created additional pressure on companies to innovate (Figure 3.1).

This graph illustrates three successive innovation waves: VHS rental, DVD by mail, and video streaming, as well as the shifting fortunes of companies such as Blockbuster and Netflix. In the 1980s and 1990s, Blockbuster dominated the VHS rental market, reaching a peak valuation

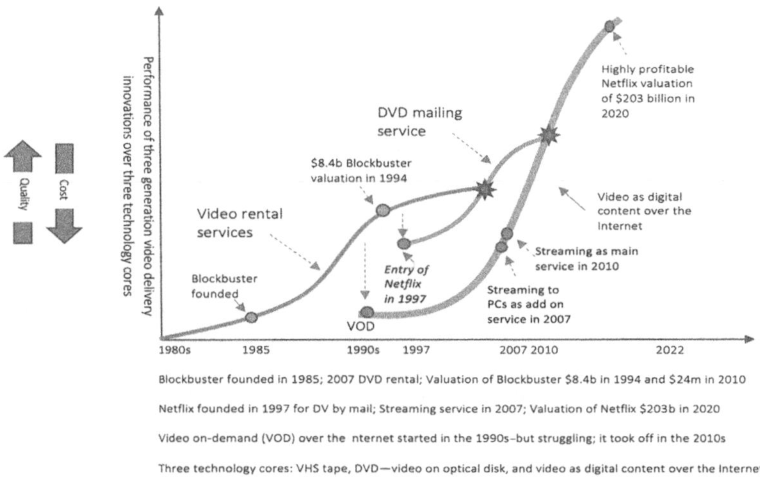

Figure 3.1 Netflix disruptive innovation—Renting to streaming

Source: The Waves, "Netflix Disruptive Innovation—Renting to Streaming," March 15, 2022.

of $8.4 billion in 1994. However, as the DVD format emerged and Internet-based video-on-demand became viable, new players like Netflix entered the market in 1997 with a more agile, customer-centric model. The real turning point came in the 2000s, when streaming over the Internet enabled even greater convenience and scalability. Netflix embraced this shift, launching its streaming service in 2007 and making it the company's core offering by 2010. Blockbuster, by contrast, failed to adapt to the new technology core and lost relevance, which culminated in its 2010 bankruptcy. Netflix, meanwhile, soared to a $203 billion valuation by 2020, and as of mid-2025 it has a market cap of nearly $500 billion.

Blockbuster, once a titan in the home entertainment industry with over 9,000 stores worldwide, is, in fact, one of the most infamous examples of failure to innovate. In 2000, Blockbuster had the opportunity to acquire Netflix for $50 million, but it declined, dismissing the idea of online streaming as a niche market. Instead, Blockbuster clung to its brick-and-mortar business model. **This story of Blockbuster's fall is so well-known that, as I write these lines, the company's last store, in Bend, Oregon, has become a tourist attraction of the old business model.**

Nokia, Kodak, and Yahoo were other leaders in their respective fields that failed to innovate and were unable to recognize emerging trends. Their failure, like Blockbuster's, can be traced to their focus on internal innovation and inability to see beyond internal biases. This inability to see beyond bias is evident, for example, in the case of Microsoft, which, although it has since recovered, struggled due to its failure to adapt to changes in the smartphone industry.

This is exemplified in Microsoft's Steve Ballmer quote from 2007, in which, in an interview before the first iPhone was launched, and Microsoft's Windows Phone was still the leading phone operating system, he said: "$500? Fully Subsidized? That is the most expensive phone in the world, and it doesn't appeal to business customers because it doesn't have a keyboard, which makes it not a very good email machine." Years later, Ballmer admitted that he didn't understand Apple's innovative model at the time.

There are, of course, many examples of successful innovation during the same period, when open innovation was forming its roots from theory to practical steps. In 2000, Procter & Gamble's new CEO, Alan G. Lafley, recognized that the company needed to reinvent itself and introduced the concept of a "connect and development" model, which involved adopting promising ideas and applying them within the company. This innovation program is still ongoing, and in 2024, the company noted that its open innovation program, "Connect + Develop," allowed it to innovate far beyond what it could do on its own. In fact, research conducted in October 2024 found that this approach has successfully increased research and development productivity at the company by some 60 percent. This program was responsible for several new products for the company, including Olay Regenerist, Swiffer Dusters, and Crest SpinBrush.

The next couple of years also presented another area in which open innovation excels: dealing with crises. These serve as a turning point for organizations. When organizations face moments of uncertainty or disruption—whether as a result of a health crisis like COVID-19, economic downturns, security threats, or trade disruptions such as tariffs and trade wars—the pressure to act sparks a unique combination of urgency, focus, and creativity. It requires companies to rethink long-standing processes, identify inefficiencies, and move faster than ever before. In these moments, barriers that once slowed progress, such as bureaucracy, hesitation, and risk aversion, disappear and are replaced by a shared drive to survive and thrive.

Crises expose weaknesses and highlight opportunities, empowering businesses to embrace bold ideas and find new sources of value. History has shown that some of the most groundbreaking innovations emerge during times of crisis.

From my experience, innovation acts as a kind of "vaccine" against crises. A crisis always accelerates innovation, but why wait? It is better to innovate today, build resilience in advance, and arrive at the crisis stronger and better positioned than the competition, thereby being ready to take the lead.

It is also vital for you, the reader, to understand that **we are already deep in a state of ongoing crisis**, which is not necessarily a geopolitical or a financial one but instead **stems from the accelerating pace of change itself. Competitors are adopting innovation faster, technology enables rapid shifts, and those who fail to keep up are already experiencing a**

crisis of relevance. This is what happened to Blockbuster, and this is what may happen to your organization if you do not act now and innovate.

This urgency is reflected in how organizations are adjusting their innovation strategies during periods of macroeconomic uncertainty.[10] According to the BCG,[11] a significant share of companies is planning to increase spending on key innovation vehicles despite potential downturns, inflation, or market instability. For example, 35 percent of organizations expect to increase investment in mergers and acquisitions, 33 percent in digital and innovation labs, 32 percent in open innovation ecosystems, and 33 percent in R&D labs. Even traditionally cost-sensitive mechanisms, such as accelerators (26 percent), corporate venture capital funds (23 percent), and incubators (22 percent) show meaningful commitment to increased spending. The majority of firms intend to at least maintain their current investment levels, signaling that innovation is viewed as a strategic necessity rather than a discretionary expense.

The 2008 economic crisis is an example of such a crisis that has resulted in innovation. Not only was the relative lack of innovation among businesses in the United States at the time considered a key factor that led to the crisis,[12] but the crisis also led to a rise in the importance of open innovation, as well as to the establishment of many start-ups that quickly became unicorns.

Organizations facing the crisis responded through an external search to adapt to changing environmental conditions, fostering increased innovation performance.[13] This period was particularly notable for innovation in the fintech industry, and **the 2008 economic crisis is considered a turning point**, resulting in the emergence of new innovative players in the financial services industry, as well as profound changes and disruptions that led to a revolution in the sector.[14]

---

[10] Boston Consulting Group. (2023, May). Most innovative companies 2023: Reaching new heights in uncertain times.

[11] Boston Consulting Group, "BCG Global Innovation Survey 2023."

[12] A. Hausman and W. J. Johnston, "The Role of Innovation in Driving the Economy: Lessons from the Global Financial Crisis," *Journal of Business Research* 67 no. 1 (2014): 2720–2726.

[13] K. Trantopoulos, M. Woerter, and G. von Krogh, "Open Innovation During the 2008 Financial Crisis," *Industry and Innovation* 31, no. 2 (2024): 159–182.

[14] D. W. Arner, J. Barberis, and R. P. Buckley, "The Evolution of Fintech: A New Post-Crisis Paradigm," *Georgetown Journal of International Law* 47 (2015): 1271.

Bold and innovative entrepreneurship can be the force that propels an organization forward, or the one that overtakes it completely. Companies that fail to innovate when things get rough will be left behind.

The 2008 crisis is one example, and while there were many catalysts for open innovation, none was as influential as COVID-19.[15] This global health crisis accelerated collaboration across industries as companies, governments, and researchers worked not only to develop vaccines and treatments at an unprecedented speed but to adjust to a changed world. **This urgency brought one critical insight to the forefront: Time to market is everything. Even organizations with unlimited resources cannot buy time.** This is a commodity that no amount of money can purchase, and during a crisis, it is the scarcest and most valuable asset of all.

At the same time, COVID-19 highlighted the necessity of open innovation in tackling complex global challenges, reinforcing the idea that collaboration is essential for rapid problem-solving, especially in light of common and cross-border crises, including economic, health, and environmental crises. Individuals, companies, and governments simply cannot do it alone and must collaborate.

Current and future crises will likely result in increased innovation for many of the same reasons. At the time of writing this book, the world is currently facing a new trade war that is likely to impact economies worldwide. This trade war and tariffs are likely to result in increased innovation and collaboration by both governments and corporations, similar to what we have seen with both the 2008 financial crisis and COVID-19.

It is not surprising, considering this current crisis, that in a recent survey of 1,039 companies worldwide, the largest share of respondents identified the ability to innovate as the most important strategic factor for generating growth over the coming 12 months.[16] Additionally, top economic performers signaled that they intend to allocate even more resources to open innovation levers than their peers.

---

[15] I. Green, "Innovation Management. The Day After the COVID-19," April 14, 2020.

[16] M. de Jong, M. Banholzer, R. Doherty, and L. LaBerge. "How Top Performers Use Innovation to Grow Within and Beyond the Core." *McKinsey Quarterly*, February 2025.

Such events and crises highlight that organizations employing open innovation strategies tend to achieve higher innovation success rates, which is only logical, since by leveraging external expertise, companies increase their likelihood of producing relevant and impactful innovation, while lowering costs and improving time to market, allowing themselves to be tomorrow's Netflix, rather than today's Blockbuster.

Unsurprisingly, most organizations today see many external stakeholders as players that should be included in the innovation process, and data[17] show that the perceived importance of different external players is consistently high: Labs are considered important by 75 percent of organizations, university collaborations matter to 78 percent, and suppliers are key for 88 percent. Incubators and accelerators, as well as start-up companies, are seen as important by 67 percent and 73 percent of organizations, respectively. The clear takeaway is that success hinges on an approach that strategically leverages a broad and diverse range of external partners. Ultimately, by understanding that valuable insights reside outside of company walls, organizations are moving beyond siloed R&D and embracing an inherently collaborative future.

Current industry practices clearly demonstrate this shift: In fact, according to a recent survey conducted in Europe, 72 percent of corporates have already launched Open Innovation projects, focusing on collaboration with start-ups, with some 50 percent of corporate–start-up collaborations initiated during or after the COVID-19 pandemic.[18]

---

[17]Sopra Steria Scale, "Open Innovation Report 2023," March 30, 2023.
[18]Ibid.

CHAPTER 4

Defining Open Innovation

No matter how big you are, no matter how good you are, you can't do it all alone.

—Professor Henry Chesbrough

As presented by Professor Chesbrough in his popular 2003 book *Open Innovation*, open innovation focuses on valuable ideas that come from outside of organizational boundaries, while considering external ideas and external paths to market at the same level of importance as those previously reserved only for internal ones. While open innovation does not mean that there is no room for internal innovation, it considers it as insufficient today, acknowledging that it is unlikely to be sufficient ever again.

In his 2006 publication, New Puzzles and New Findings, Professor Chesbrough modified his original definition of open innovation: "Open innovation is the use of purposive inflows and outflows of knowledge to accelerate internal innovation and expand the markets for external use of innovation, respectively,"[19] stressing the importance of knowledge inflows and outflows.

Finally, this definition was revised again by Chesbrough and Bogers in 2014, stating that open innovation is a distributed innovation process based on purposefully managed knowledge flows across organizational boundaries, utilizing both pecuniary and nonpecuniary mechanisms in line with the organization's business model.[20]

---

[19]H. Chesbrough, "New Puzzles and New Findings," in *Open Innovation: Researching a New Paradigm,* ed. Henry Chesbrough, Joel West, and Wim Vanhaverbeke (Oxford University Press, 2006), 15–33.

[20]H. Chesbrough and M. Bogers, "Explicating Open Innovation: Clarifying an Emerging Paradigm for Understanding Innovation, in *New Frontiers in Open Innovation*, ed. Henry Chesbrough, Joel West, and Wim Vanhaverbeke (Oxford University Press, 2014), 3–28.

The evolution of definitions underscores the basic common principle: **The linear, closed innovation model is no longer sufficient, and organizations cannot successfully innovate in isolation.** Instead, organizations must collaborate with a broad range of external partners, such as start-ups, universities, other companies, and so on, to remain ahead of the competition.

The traditional R&D process, often described as a "closed" model, requires organizations to invest heavily in building and maintaining internal teams, labs, and intellectual property, prioritizing control and secrecy. While this approach has strengths, including safeguarding proprietary technologies and ensuring tight integration with corporate strategy, it also has substantial drawbacks. It is resource-intensive, slow-moving, and often disconnected from the broader innovation ecosystem.

In contrast, open innovation transcends organizational boundaries. It is a boundary-spanning approach that actively seeks external contributions and partnerships to cocreate value. **Unlike the linear, hierarchical nature of traditional R&D, open innovation thrives on collaboration, flexibility, and adaptability.** This dynamic framework allows organizations to integrate external ideas into their processes while simultaneously sharing their intellectual property with external entities for mutual benefit (Figure 4.1).

While closed innovation is characterized by an organization investing hundreds of millions of dollars and years of effort to develop a new

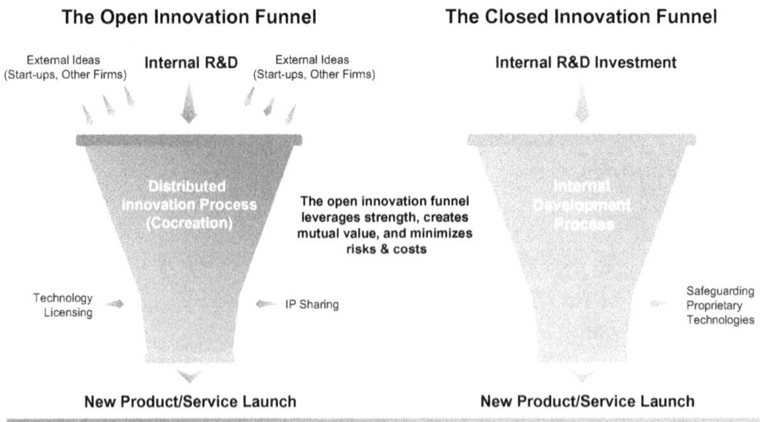

Figure 4.1 Comparing open and closed innovation funnels

product in-house, through open innovation, that same company might partner with a start-up that already has a solution in development or license a technology from a university to achieve the needed solution more effectively. This results in a considerably faster time to market, while also minimizing risks and costs.

MaxTech Networks is a great example of this. The company, which had 20 employees at the time, managed to raise $20 million and, within a short time, developed a working MESH-based communication device, which establishes an independent communication network. At the same time, a large corporation, HLS, with over 10,000 employees, invested hundreds of millions of dollars over an extended period, involving hundreds of engineers, yet failed to produce a functioning product on the same MESH technology. The two companies began to meet every quarter, and each time, the corporation's VP of R&D was astonished to see how MaxTech, with far fewer resources, had advanced further than their own teams.

Despite MaxTech's many offers to collaborate, through white labeling or a cobranding agreement in exchange for licensing fees, the corporation rejected the opportunity to leverage its vast sales, financial, and marketing capabilities to scale the MaxTech solution. Instead, quarter after quarter, the company's VP met with the CEO and asked for additional funds and more staff to compete with MaxTech.

In 2018, the technology was put to the test. A high-profile rescue mission of 12 boys and their coach, who were trapped in a cave in Thailand, required a way to communicate in an area with no infrastructure. MaxTech and HLS both arrived at the cave entrance with their communication devices. Shockingly (to some...) MaxTech's product was the only one that worked. As a result, MaxTech was featured on CNN, while HLS lost contracts worth hundreds of millions of dollars across Southeast Asia.

This is a great example of the efficiency of start-ups and of why corporations must work with others, leveraging each other's strengths, while creating mutual value. This has implications across industries, and today, with advanced technology, it is possible to start a bank or insurance company, for example, based on modern infrastructure, faster and at a lower cost compared to legacy companies that still rely on outdated core systems.

In 2007, Chesbrough and Appleyard[21] noted that organizations were adopting this new model of innovation but acknowledged that shifting from ownership over ideas to the pooling of knowledge requires companies to rethink their strategy, and that organizations are now grappling with value capture and sustainability of their business models. It is simply not enough to collaborate; instead, you have to know how to do it, and you must learn how to best take advantage of this model and all it has to offer.

Recent data collected by Stewart Mehlman and the Innovation Research Interchange[22] reinforce this reality, showing a clear and ongoing commitment among organizations to external collaboration. According to the findings, the majority of collaboration types are experiencing net increases. For example, 57 percent of organizations report increased participation in R&D alliances, 30 percent report growth in R&D consortia, and 30 percent note increases in contracts or grants with academia. Collaboration with government labs is also rising, with 25 percent of organizations expanding such partnerships. Engagement with start-ups shows particularly strong momentum, with 34 percent of respondents increasing their collaboration activities.

Even categories such as outbound IP licensing (14 percent), crowdsourcing or open innovation competitions (14 percent), and corporate venture capital (16 percent) demonstrate meaningful upward trends. Across most collaboration types, only a small minority report decreases—indicating that external innovation partnerships are not only widespread but expanding.

In the Israeli ecosystem, for example, we have seen a rapid growth in open innovation, with a notable rise in the number of open innovation teams deployed by multinational corporations. This rise has been steady since 2014.

An ecosystem mapping of the Israeli ecosystem[23] highlights just how rapidly open innovation models are expanding, particularly in Israel,

---

[21] H. W. Chesbrough and M. M. Appleyard, "Open Innovation and Strategy," *California Management Review* 50, no. 1 (2007): 57–76.

[22] S. Mehlman, "2024 R&D Trends Forecast: Results from the Innovation Research Interchange's Annual Survey," *Research-Technology Management* 67, no. 1 (2024): 22–33.

[23] "PwC & Start-Up Nation Central MNC Ecosystem Mapping," 2019.

where 536 multinational corporations operate innovation activities. Their analysis shows that while R&D-led models still dominate at 59 percent, partnership-led models already account for 25 percent of innovation activity, and investment-led models make up an additional 16 percent. This distribution underscores a clear shift: open, partnership-driven innovation models are growing faster than traditional approaches.

And yet, external collaboration is not enough, and for it to succeed, open innovation requires several pillars to innovate successfully: **culture, leadership, strategy, structures, human capital, and external relations**, all of which will be discussed in more detail throughout the book. Still, for now, you must understand that **successfully navigating this complexity requires companies to recognize and engage with the diverse stakeholders of the innovation ecosystem**, including corporations, start-ups, academia, and government entities.

Understanding the interplay between these and how to harness their distinct added value is key to driving impactful results.

CHAPTER 5

Mapping the Innovation Ecosystem

No matter who you are, most of the smartest people work for someone else.

—Bill Joy, Venture Capitalist and Cofounder of Sun Microsystems

Innovation thrives in ecosystems, which are dynamic networks of interconnected players that contribute their unique strengths to foster breakthroughs and drive progress and value. Understanding and mapping these ecosystems is essential for organizations wishing to innovate successfully.

In the context of innovation, an ecosystem is a network of entities such as corporations, start-ups, universities, governments, investors, and more, that collaborate and compete to create and implement new ideas, technologies, and solutions.

Innovation ecosystems are similar to biological ecosystems, where various species interact in a shared environment to thrive and survive. Companies today should not be viewed as members of a single industry but as part of a broader ecosystem across multiple industries, working together to achieve shared goals. Here, each player has a unique role to play, contributing resources, knowledge, and expertise to drive collective progress, while working both cooperatively and competitively to support new products, satisfy customer needs, and incorporate innovation.[24]

A good example of an ecosystem player could be a traditional bank, typically seen as part of the finance industry, and it alone. In reality, it is an organization with many different aspects, including service,

[24]J. F. Moore, "Predators and Prey: A New Ecology of Competition," *Harvard Business Review* 71, no. 3 (1993): 75–86.

marketing, legal, human resources, finance, operations, and more, making its required areas of innovation and interest far broader than financial services. Relevant ecosystems depend, therefore, on the business sectors and internal operations, which differ from organization to organization, even within the same industry.

It is essential to understand that each member of the ecosystem ultimately shares the fate of the ecosystem, regardless of the member's own strength. This emphasizes that companies cannot solely focus on their internal capabilities but must also promote the overall health of their ecosystem,[25] precisely because **of an ecosystem's unique ability to amplify the innovation potential of all its participants operating within it**. As stated before, no single entity can successfully navigate today's changing technological landscape alone. As a result, organizations work together within ecosystems that foster collaboration, cocreation, and knowledge sharing to address today's complex problems in this new reality in which knowledge flows across organizational boundaries, industries, and regions.

Beyond ideation and implementation, ecosystems are also essential to understanding where the winds of innovation are currently blowing, and organizations often learn more effectively about market trends when they meet such players as start-ups and learn from them about the trends. This is usually much more effective than hiring business intelligence providers or strategic consultancy firms.

Ecosystems are particularly essential for resilience and adaptability. In times of chaos, such as economic downturns or global crises, ecosystems provide the agility to pivot quickly. A corporation facing challenges might find solutions by partnering with a start-up that has already developed the necessary tools or technology.

Similarly, governments can support ecosystems during crises by funding innovation programs, ensuring continuity and future growth. A fantastic example is the Israeli Ministry of Defense, which, in response to the events following October 7, collaborated with start-ups to deploy or develop life-saving solutions, including tourniquets and water purification systems, and addressed critical logistical issues. One notable case is Corsight AI, which develops advanced Face Intelligence technology that

[25]Iansiti and Levien, "Strategy as Ecology," 68–81.

delivers real-time insights to enhance safety, efficiency, and decision making across diverse sectors, including law enforcement, critical infrastructure, health care, retail, and transportation. Built on an ethical foundation with privacy by design, Corsight's technology is used worldwide to help organizations turn visual data into actionable intelligence while upholding the highest standards of responsibility and transparency.

During the October 7 terror attack in Israel, and its aftermath, Corsight's existing capabilities were adapted to support urgent national needs, one of many examples demonstrating how its technology can be mobilized in times of crisis. According to media reports, their solution was initially deployed in Gaza to locate Israelis abducted by Hamas during the October 7 terror attack.

It is worth noting that previously, the relevant state authorities were unfamiliar with Corsight and its technological potential. The connection was established after an urgent challenge was sent by a group of Israeli entrepreneurs (face recognition of wounded Israeli civilians and soldiers), which prompted me to introduce Corsight to the relevant officials.

As Israel launched a ground offensive, the technology was increasingly used to identify suspects affiliated with Hamas or other terror groups and to enhance the clarity of drone footage. Following this initial success, the Ministry of Defense and other agencies leveraged Corsight's rapid responsiveness and proven accuracy, integrating it into dozens of projects that required fast and precise identification.

This case exemplifies the versatility and societal value of Israel's innovation ecosystem, how technologies like Corsight's can serve both public safety and civil applications with integrity and measurable impact, and how ecosystems are not only economic engines for corporations and governments but also serve as strategic assets in times of emergency or crisis—even at the national level.

The screenshot I am sharing here shows the importance of this technology (Figure 5.1):

This story of Corsight highlights a deeper truth about innovation ecosystems: Their power is not only in individual technologies but in the dynamic structure that enables rapid connection, adaptation, and collaboration during critical moments. Innovation ecosystems, much like biological ones, are constantly evolving. To understand why some ecosystems,

Were you able to help?

We identified all of them yesterday.

Shai, a huge thank you for all the help today. We did a lot of good with your help and with the help of your company. We were able to bring families together with the injured or at least get some closure with the deceased . . We wouldn't have made half of it without you. Huge thanks.
I would be happy if you could pass it along to the people at your company. Really, thank you.

Figure 5.1 A testimonial on Corsight's technology

such as Israeli ones, are uniquely capable of responding quickly in times of crisis, it is helpful to look at how ecosystems grow, evolve, and mature over time.

The evolutionary stages of an innovation ecosystem can be broken down into four key stages: birth, expansion, leadership, and self-renewal.[26]

During the Birth stage, the primary focus is on defining a new value proposition around a seed innovation, which requires collaboration with customers and suppliers. At this stage, competitive challenges include protecting ideas from competitors and securing critical resources and channels. Consider a start-up in its early days, attempting to build a business ecosystem. For example, Mobileye in its early days worked closely with automotive manufacturers to prove its collision-avoidance technology, while guarding its proprietary algorithms until it could secure strategic partnerships.

The Expansion stage involves scaling new offers to a broader market by working with suppliers and partners to ensure maximum market coverage. This stage is characterized by the need to outmaneuver alternative implementations of similar ideas, establishing the market standard, and dominating key segments. Here, the start-up will continue to develop and expand partnerships with organizations, building an ecosystem around itself. A case in point is Waze, which after initial success in Israel partnered with global mapping providers, telecom companies, and automakers to expand its reach before being acquired by Google.

[26]Moore, "Predators and Prey," 75–86.

The Leadership stage aims to provide a compelling vision for the future, encouraging continuous improvement of the complete offer through cooperation with suppliers and customers. Maintaining strong bargaining power and solidifying relationships with key ecosystem players is crucial here, and through increased partnerships and collaborations, the ecosystem continues to grow in this stage, positioning some players as market leaders. For example, NVIDIA has solidified its leadership in AI hardware by fostering a robust developer ecosystem and cooperation.

Finally, the Self-Renewal stage emphasizes the importance of bringing new ideas to the existing ecosystem by collaborating with innovators and a cyclical approach that ensures the ecosystem's longevity and adaptability in a competitive market. Here, the market leader will be forced to "innovate now or die." Apple, for instance, continuously renews its ecosystem by encouraging third-party developers, acquiring start-ups in emerging fields, and integrating new technologies like augmented reality into its product roadmap.

It can be argued that while the first three stages focus on a new technology or solution, the fourth stage is more continental, and its success is based on the number of additional start-ups and collaborations within the ecosystem. Seen through this lens, the Corsight case is not an isolated example but a demonstration of an ecosystem in its self-renewing, highly adaptive phase, where new start-ups, new collaborations, and new channels of connection enable rapid responses even at the national level (Figure 5.2).

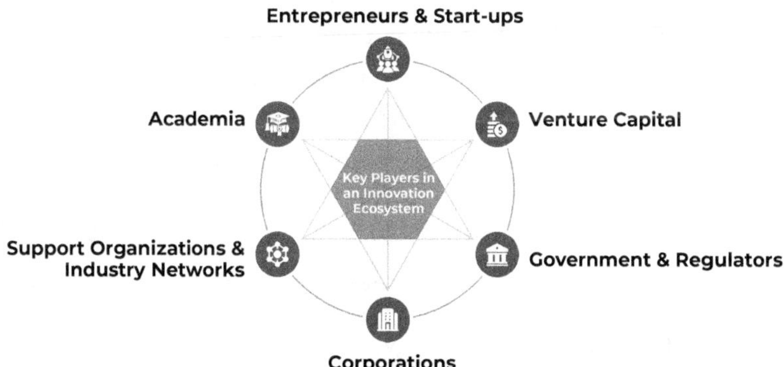

Figure 5.2 Key Players in an Innovation Ecosystem

Corporations often serve as the anchor of innovation ecosystems, providing the scale, resources, and infrastructure necessary to bring ideas to market. They have the advantage of established customer bases, supply chains, and capital, which allow them to deploy new solutions on a large scale. However, as previously mentioned, traditional corporations struggle with agility and out-of-the-box thinking, which is why engaging with external innovators is crucial for them to remain competitive. An ecosystem allows an established company to maximize its ability to develop and acquire innovation through a platform in which new ventures and smaller companies, as well as other players, contribute their innovations.[27]

Apple, IBM, Ford, Walmart, Amazon, Merck, Alibaba, and Ping An are all examples of ecosystem leaders that often collaborate with start-ups. Apple's ecosystem, for example, crosses several industries, including computers, consumer electronics, communications, and information, with an extensive web of suppliers, customers, and other collaborators.

These leaders, or keystones,[28] may represent a small part of the ecosystem but still exert tremendous influence. These organizations play a crucial role in their ecosystems and improve and stabilize them while increasing ecosystem productivity by connecting network participants to one another. These organizations are crucial to an ecosystem, and their demise may potentially lead to the catastrophic collapse of the entire system. With that said, these players, like all members of the ecosystem, are not altruistic, and they collaborate and support their fellow members because open innovation is beneficial to all members of the ecosystem, including themselves.

Innovation ecosystems are not new and have been around for several decades. For example, Companies like Intel and IBM created robust innovation ecosystems in the 1980s and the 1990s. With that said, compared to the late twentieth century, innovation ecosystems are no longer restricted to technological players and have become widespread not only across industries but across regions, allowing companies from around the world to participate in innovation and value-creation opportunities.[29]

---

[27]S. A. Zahra and S. Nambisan, "Entrepreneurship in Global Innovation Ecosystems," *AMS Review* 1 (2011): 4–17.

[28]Iansiti and Levien, "Strategy as Ecology," 68–81.

[29]Zahra and Nambisan, "Entrepreneurship in Global Innovation Ecosystems," 4–17.

Ping An is a standout example of an ecosystem leader, demonstrating how a long-term strategy can revolutionize an industry. Over some 20 years, Ping An evolved from a traditional insurer operating in China, into a diversified powerhouse, leveraging technology to deliver value across multiple sectors. The company has built a comprehensive ecosystem integrating its core insurance business with adjacent fields such as health care, finance, real estate, smart city solutions, and automotive services. Ping An has created an interconnected network of services that not only addresses customer needs but also generates vast amounts of data to enhance its risk management and product offerings, positioning the company as a leader in its industry.

In 2020, Ping An's ecosystem was structured around several verticals, particularly FinTech, HealthTech, Real Estate Tech, Auto Tech, Cloud Tech, and Smart City, each supported by vertical accelerators designed to onboard relevant start-ups and codevelop solutions tailored to the needs of Ping An's subsidiaries. These accelerators helped the company strengthen the competitiveness of each vertical, explore collaborations with global partners, and scale innovation across the entire ecosystem. The model enabled Ping An to consistently integrate new technologies, deepen cross-sector capabilities, and rapidly pilot innovations in collaboration with external partners.

One effective way to share knowledge between corporations is through **accelerators**, where international players with similar areas of interest collaborate. For instance, IBM's AlphaZone accelerator included 10 international partners from the insurance industry. This accelerator facilitated knowledge sharing between companies and created connections between the insurers and the start-up participants, leading to implementations and successful investments.

Connections such as these also lead to business partnerships that could not have happened without the "excuse" provided by innovation. Here, for instance, thanks to IBM's platform, these international insurance companies, many of which had never engaged directly in such a manner before, began meaningful conversations with each other, jointly evaluating start-ups, discussing emerging trends, and exploring potential collaborations.

Another good example from the insurance industry is Munich Re Digital Partners, which partners with insurtechs, fintechs, and even mature companies to innovate and digitize the insurance industry.

Consider how the Silicon Valley operates as an ecosystem: venture capital, universities (such as Stanford), start-ups, and tech giants (such as Apple and Google) coexist in a shared space, exchanging talent, insights, and resources, all working together to drive technological advancements and economic growth.

In Israel, for example, for over a decade now, there has been a quarterly meeting where innovation leaders from international corporations gather to share knowledge regarding deal flow and emerging trends. While this might sound as risk of giving away a company's advantage points, this type of collaboration is actually valuable to all participants, as it fosters a shared understanding of the market without disclosing proprietary secrets, and **allows participants to exchange opinions on entrepreneurs, trends, deal flows, as well as the prospects of new technologies, saving time and ensuring that companies stay ahead of the curve** by leveraging collective expertise, while also resulting in potential coinvestments.

Lessons Learned from Corporate Giants and Their Start-Up Collaborations: eBay and Skype

In 2005, eBay acquired Skype for $2.6 billion, believing that integrating voice communication into its auction platform would enhance buyer-seller interactions.

However, the integration of Skype into eBay's platform faced significant challenges, from a lack of a clear use case for voice communication among eBay users to a strategic misalignment between the two companies. The acquisition was also criticized for being overpriced, given Skype's revenue was only $7 million.

What Went Wrong?

1. There was no clear use case. While eBay assumed that voice communication would improve online commerce, users preferred text-based messaging. There was also no strategic fit, as Skype did not align with eBay's core business.

2. The purchase price of $2.6 billion was considered high given Skype's revenue and growth stage at the time. This placed excessive pressure on the collaboration to deliver outsized results quickly, resulting in tension and unrealistic expectations that further undermined the partnership's success.
3. eBay lacked a comprehensive plan to integrate Skype into its business structure, leading to operational challenges.

Successful examples can be seen in initiatives like Microsoft's partnerships with AI start-ups or Johnson & Johnson's JLABS, which provide support and funding for health-focused entrepreneurs. Microsoft, for example, has been actively fostering innovation by partnering with AI start-ups through initiatives such as the Microsoft Founders Hub, which offers start-ups free access to advanced AI models along with personalized guidance to accelerate their growth and integration of AI technologies, as well as Microsoft's investments in OpenAI, which **provided the latter with the funds needed to bring OpenAI to what it is today while providing Microsoft some control and the ability to deploy AI early throughout its products and services**, including Office and GitHub.

Johnson & Johnson's JLABS is another excellent example. It is a global network of life science incubators designed to support health care entrepreneurs, operating under a "no-strings-attached" model. This provides start-ups access to state-of-the-art lab space, equipment, and resources without taking equity or imposing intellectual property constraints. At the same time, they also offer funding, investor connections, and more, allowing for industry innovation and mutual benefit.

Corporations provide the following benefits to the ecosystem:

1. Market Insights: Established companies have a deep understanding of market dynamics and customer needs. This knowledge can guide the development of products and improve product–market fit.
2. Scale and Distribution: Corporations can leverage their existing distribution networks to bring new innovations to market quickly and efficiently, ensuring successful ideas reach consumers faster. Additionally, they bring their existing customers and operations with them.

3. Funding and Resources: Corporations can provide significant financial backing for research and development initiatives, enabling innovative projects that might be too risky for smaller entities.
4. Unique Challenges: Perhaps the most important thing corporations bring to the table is their unique set of challenges. As soon as entrepreneurs are faced with corporate challenges, they come up with creative solutions to these challenges that are relevant to the corporation's needs.

Lessons Learned from Corporate Giants and Their Start-Up Collaborations: Ford and Rivian

The transition to electric vehicles has forced traditional automakers to reassess their approach to innovation. Ford, recognizing the need for a faster route into the EV market, invested $500 million in Rivian in 2019 to codevelop a new electric vehicle.

The partnership was later terminated as Ford developed confidence in its own EV technology, particularly with its Mustang Mach-E and F-150 Lightning proving successful in the market. Meanwhile, Rivian, after receiving a massive investment from Amazon and focusing on its product roadmap, found itself less reliant on Ford as a strategic partner.

The collaboration failed to produce a joint product, showing that corporate priorities can shift quickly even when partnerships begin with strong alignment.

Lessons Learned:

1. Strategic alignment must be reassessed as both companies evolve. Ford and Rivian started aligned, but their paths diverged.
2. Financial investment does not guarantee product collaboration.
3. Corporate partnerships with start-ups require clear exit strategies, and companies must be ready to pivot when external partnerships no longer serve their strategic goals.

Start-ups represent the driving force of agility and creativity in the ecosystem. Unencumbered by bureaucratic processes, start-ups can experiment, iterate, and pivot quickly. They are often the first to explore emerging technologies and take risks that larger companies cannot. Start-ups contribute fresh ideas and disruptive solutions that can challenge industry norms. For example, fintech start-ups have revolutionized the banking sector, especially after the 2008 economic crisis, with such solutions as mobile payments, lending platforms, and blockchain technology innovations. **While start-ups often lack the resources and reach of large corporations, partnerships with corporate players can provide them with the funding, guidance, and access needed to scale their ideas.**

Their unique contributions, therefore, include:

1. Disruptive Ideas: Start-ups frequently challenge established norms with innovative solutions that can disrupt traditional industries. Their fresh perspectives and new ideas lead to novel approaches that larger companies may overlook or fail to implement without collaboration. It is likely that a disruptive idea like Airbnb, for example, would not have emerged from within a traditional hotel chain.
2. Flexibility: Unlike large corporations, start-ups can pivot quickly in response to market feedback, emerging trends, and major crises. Figuratively, a start-up can be imagined as a racing boat, while a corporation resembles an aircraft carrier—the latter cannot change direction easily when needed. This adaptability allows start-ups to explore uncharted territories in technology and business models while pivoting to achieve product–market fit. DigitalOwl (formerly Legal Automation), for example, started as a tech solution for the legal domain. Once they met with insurance companies, they decided to shift their offering to the financial sector. The company, backed by angel investor Amnon Shashua, uses advanced AI to read, analyze, and summarize medical records for insurance claims, at a speed and accuracy unattainable by humans, enabling insurers to make faster and more informed decisions.
3. Entrepreneurial Spirit: The culture of risk-taking, which is inherent in start-ups, fosters an environment where creativity flourishes. This entrepreneurial mindset is essential for driving radical innovations,

as they are the ecosystem's most energetic, hardworking, and technologically up-to-date players. When organizations hire employees with a start-up background, the organization's DNA becomes more aligned with the times. Such employees bring in a new spirit, essential for innovation, allowing corporations to remain competitive.

Universities serve as another important player, providing the foundation of knowledge and discovery within the innovation ecosystem. **Universities and research institutions are at the forefront of technology, offering a steady pipeline of intellectual capital and technological advancements.** These players serve as incubators of new ideas, producing research that start-ups and corporations can later commercialize. MIT's Media Lab, for instance, is an interdisciplinary research lab that has been a powerhouse of innovation since 1985, spawning technologies that have transformed industries, often through start-ups and corporations. This lab was responsible for developments such as e-Ink technology, the first wearable technology prototypes, the technology behind augmented reality, and many of the foundations used by cryptocurrency today.

Their contributions include:

1. Cutting-Edge Research: Universities conduct fundamental research that leads to groundbreaking discoveries. Their research often forms the basis for new technologies that can later be commercialized. For example, the development of the Internet originated from research at institutions like MIT and Stanford, and later by work done by the U.S. Department of Defense. Similarly, advancements in quantum computing, many of which stem from university-led initiatives, are now moving toward commercial applications.
2. Talent Development: Universities produce a skilled workforce equipped with the knowledge and expertise necessary for driving innovation, and graduates often become key players in start-ups or corporate R&D teams. Beyond technical expertise, universities also cultivate future managers and entrepreneurs. For instance, INSEAD was an early pioneer in integrating entrepreneurship into its MBA curriculum, and Stanford University has long been a global benchmark for fostering start-up culture through programs

like the Stanford Technology Ventures Program. Reichman University is another example of a university that hosts a dedicated faculty for entrepreneurship. These examples highlight the academic world's role in shaping not only technologists but also business leaders and innovators.

3. Knowledge Transfer: Collaborations between academia and industry facilitate the transfer of knowledge from research settings to practical applications. For example, the Hebrew University of Jerusalem operates technology transfer initiatives, such as "Yissum," which connects academic research with commercial partners, facilitating the successful commercialization of innovations across various fields, including agriculture, medicine, and AI. This is a common practice among many leading universities, translating theoretical advancements into practical solutions.

Governments play a dual role in the ecosystem, as both regulators and enablers. On the one hand, regulators establish policies and frameworks that govern innovation activities, ensuring ethical standards, data privacy, and fair competition. At the same time, they also act as catalysts for innovation by providing funding, infrastructure, and incentives, resulting in a particularly crucial role.

The Startup Nation provides a notable example with Dr. Hedva Ber, the former supervisor of banks, who introduced comprehensive directives to promote innovation and digitization in the banking system, including a wide range of complementary reforms: enabling customers to access all banking services digitally and remotely; requiring banks to offer digital literacy training, especially for seniors; leading the open banking reform, which allows customers to control and share their own financial data; authorizing the transition of banks to cloud technologies; supporting digital payment infrastructures; and removing barriers to establish Israel's first fully digital bank, One Zero, after four decades without a new banking license. More broadly, under her leadership, the Banking Supervision Department defined innovation and digitization as strategic objectives aimed at improving service and enhancing competition. Finally, in 2018, she not only required every bank to appoint a director with expertise in innovation and technology but also instructed them to establish a dedicated

Technology and Innovation Committee. This committee was designed to accompany banks in their digital transformation processes and to discuss both emerging opportunities and risks. Dr. Ber was a pioneer in this regard, demonstrating how regulators can lead with foresight rather than follow change. Her actions serve as an inspiration for regulators worldwide, demonstrating the importance of looking far ahead, which she truly did. This raises an important question: Why should companies wait for a regulator to make such moves?

Programs such as Horizon Europe and the Small Business Innovation Research program, administered by the U.S. government, both exemplify how governments can support start-ups and academic research while fostering collaboration with more established industry players. Additionally, governments can set national innovation agendas.

One example can be seen within the Israeli ecosystem, where a network of companies and talent emerged, including Check Point and CyberArk. Here, the government played a key role in supporting and nurturing the ecosystem's growth through targeted incentives, grants, and policy measures, fostering dozens of start-ups that collaborated with Israeli corporations and the government. This ecosystem is well-supported by the Israeli military, with many developments stemming from military-developed technologies and know-how transferred into the civilian sphere. Many of Israel's cyber start-ups were founded by alums of elite intelligence units such as Unit 8200, where advanced capabilities developed for national defense were later adapted to serve commercial needs. Similar forward-looking government support can be seen today in areas such as AI and quantum computing, where proactive policies and investments aim to cultivate emerging ecosystems even before they have reached mainstream maturity.

Another good example is the Portuguese government's initiative to establish and promote the traveltech ecosystem through founding NEST, the Tourism Innovation Centre. Other examples include South Korea's emphasis on green technologies and the British focus on fintech. This is done to align ecosystem efforts with long-term strategic goals by governments.

Additionally, governments periodically identify sectors that require nurturing and are not adequately advanced by the market and invest in these areas. In Israel, for example, several government-backed incubator programs have been recently launched, focusing on fields previously under the radar but of significant importance. The incubators were formed due to the understanding that a government cannot lead developments in such fields as chips, bioconvergence, agri-foodtech, robotics, defense tech, and other fields characterized by high technological complexity without collaboration with start-ups, universities, and corporations.

Governments also play a critical role in de-risking investments to encourage private-sector participation. For example, when the government guarantees a minimum return on an investment portfolio, committing to compensate investors if returns fall below a certain threshold, it creates a more attractive alternative investment channel than traditional options. This mechanism incentivizes investments in innovation-driven sectors that might otherwise be perceived as too risky. These types of activities are not something new in Israel, and in 1993, Israel first introduced the "Yozma" program, which jumpstarted Israeli venture capital by matching funds invested by foreign investors .In recent years, the Israeli government has launched additional initiatives such as the 2020 "Track 43" incentive program, which offered institutional investors protection of up to 40 percent against losses in the value of their portfolio, making investment in innovative ventures far more attractive. Another great example is the "Angels Law," designed to encourage private investments by offering tax benefits to individual investors who support early-stage start-ups.

To summarize, major governmental contributions include:

1. Policy Frameworks: Governments create regulatory environments that either foster or hinder innovation. Supportive policies can encourage entrepreneurship, protect intellectual property rights, and promote investment in research.
2. Funding Opportunities: Public funding programs often provide grants or subsidies for innovative projects, particularly in sectors deemed strategically important for national interests (e.g., health care, renewable energy).
3. Infrastructure Development: Governments invest in infrastructure that supports innovation ecosystems, such as technology parks,

incubators, and research facilities. These investments create environments conducive to collaboration among various stakeholders.

Finally, investors and risk capital serve in many ways as the lifeblood of innovation ecosystems, providing the financial resources necessary to transform ideas into impactful, scalable solutions. Venture capital firms, angel investors, and corporate investment arms all play a crucial role in supporting start-ups and high-risk initiatives that would otherwise struggle to secure funding through traditional means.

Beyond funding, investors also contribute significant strategic value to the ecosystem. Many bring expertise, mentorship, and industry connections, guiding ventures to refine their business models and navigate challenges. This blend of capital and know-how often catalyzes the rapid growth of start-ups and supports their integration into broader innovation ecosystems. For example, SoftBank's Vision Fund has significantly invested in emerging technologies, helping scale companies like Uber.

Likewise, Angel investors serve an important role in investing in early-stage start-ups, with 83 percent of their investment aimed at Seed and Round A rounds, while being responsible for 21 percent of all investments in Seed rounds.[30]

Importantly, risk capital providers also act as a bridge between different players in the ecosystem. They facilitate collaborations between start-ups, corporations, and academic institutions, aligning their interests and fostering synergies.

This role is further strengthened when governments implement de-risking mechanisms such as guaranteed returns or coinvestment structures. These tools lower the perceived risk for nongovernmental investors, making funding early-stage ventures and innovative technologies more viable. In doing so, governments help unlock private capital that might otherwise remain on the sidelines.

Their main contributions, therefore, include:

1. Financial Support for High-Risk Ventures: Investors provide the critical funding needed for start-ups and high-risk projects that

[30]Angel Capital Association, "Angel Funders Report 2023," 2023.

often lack access to traditional financing sources, enabling the development of innovative solutions. A great example is Fusion, Israel's most active preseed VC platform, which has backed over 130 start-ups since 2017. Its investment team, including Guy Katsovich, Yair Vardi, and Amit Shechter, writes dozens of $150,000 checks annually, often to first-time founders from underrepresented sectors, where higher risk exists. In their recent report,[31] they highlight a shift toward lower preseed valuations driven by the rise of Israeli micro-funds and increased early-stage interest from U.S. VCs willing to take more risk in exchange for higher equity.

2. Strategic Guidance and Mentorship: Many investors offer expertise, mentorship, and industry connections to help start-ups refine business models, navigate challenges, and position themselves for growth.
3. Facilitation of Ecosystem Collaboration: Risk capital providers act as connectors between start-ups, corporations, and academic institutions, fostering partnerships and aligning their efforts to maximize innovation potential.

The interactions between these stakeholders form the backbone of thriving innovation ecosystems, with corporations providing scale, start-ups bringing agility, academia offering foundational research, and governments creating enabling conditions and regulation frameworks. When these entities align their efforts, they can address complex challenges that no organization can tackle alone.

[31]Fusion VC, "The 2024 Pre-Seed Investment Landscape Report: A Survey of Active VCs and Angels," March 10, 2025.

CHAPTER 6

Global and Local Ecosystems: Challenges and Opportunities

Tough times bring out the best parts of Silicon Valley.

—Sergey Brin

Innovation ecosystems are based on the interplay between global innovation hubs and local ecosystems, each playing a vital role in driving progress. While these ecosystems can evolve on their own, **the successful ones are formed with a comprehensive, strategic approach that leverages the unique strengths of local ecosystems while taking full advantage of global networks.**

Global hubs are the epicenters of technological advancement and entrepreneurship, attracting talent and investment. Meanwhile, local ecosystems operate at the grassroots level, often developing innovations tailored to regional needs. Ecosystems thrive when local leaders and developers identify and build upon existing skill bases and institutional strengths within their regions.[32] Silicon Valley, for instance, has become synonymous with technological disruption, housing tech giants like Apple, Google, and Tesla, as well as numerous successful start-ups. Its success is rooted in a unique combination of talent concentration, venture capital networks, and a culture of risk-taking and experimentation.

[32]C. Davis, B. Safran, R. Schaff, and L. Yayboke, "Building Innovation Ecosystems: Accelerating Tech Hub Growth, *McKinsey*, February 28, 2023, https://www.mckinsey.com/industries/public-sector/our-insights/building-innovation-ecosystems-accelerating-tech-hub-growth.

Success Stories in Open Innovation: Unilever

Challenge: Unilever set ambitious sustainability goals but needed fresh ideas and cutting-edge technology.

Open Innovation Approach: The Unilever Foundry connects the company with start-ups focused on sustainable solutions, offering funding and business integration opportunities.

Outcome: The Unilever Foundry fostered over 200 partnerships, scaled about 50 percent of pilot projects, and drove innovation across various areas, including sustainability, product development, and more.

Boston is another example of such an ecosystem that has successfully leveraged its prestigious universities, Harvard and MIT, along with leading medical institutions, while cultivating a collaborative environment between academia, health care, and entrepreneurs across various sectors and industries.

According to a McKinsey,[33] Boston's innovation activity is concentrated in two major districts: Kendall Square in Cambridge and the Seaport district. These areas host a high density of innovation centers, research institutions, hospitals, education facilities, and cultural venues, all located within walkable proximity. This geographic clustering enables frequent interactions between scientists, clinicians, academics, founders, and investors, creating a fertile environment for cross-disciplinary collaboration and rapid knowledge exchange. This has made Boston a major hub for cutting-edge scientific and technological advancements.

Similarly, Shenzhen has transitioned from a manufacturing hub to a global leader in hardware innovation, with companies like Huawei and DJI. Shenzhen's dense supply chain ecosystem and government-backed incentives for tech development make it a case study in how policy and private enterprises can align to fuel innovation.

Another example is South Korea, which reached dominance in the display screen industry. Global brands like Samsung and LG did not emerge

[33]McKinsey & Company, "Place-Based Innovation Ecosystems: Boston–Cambridge Innovation Districts," *Joint Research Centre*, 2019.

by accident, and their success is rooted in decades of government-backed industrial policy, significant public and private R&D investment, and the unique structure of conglomerates. The government prioritized core strategic technologies, providing incentives and large-scale funding that enabled these companies to move from simple assembly to mastering the highly complex manufacturing processes for advanced OLED (organic light-emitting diode) and QLED (quantum-dot light-emitting diode) display panels. This model, characterized by centralized, coordinated national champions, offers a stark contrast to the decentralized, venture-capital-driven approach of Silicon Valley, demonstrating a different yet highly effective path to global ecosystem dominance.

Global hubs, however, are not without issues, and they often monopolize global resources, leaving other regions underfunded and overshadowed. Innovations emerging from global hubs may also prioritize solutions for high-income, urban markets, neglecting the specific needs of developing regions. For example, IoT-enabled home automation systems may thrive in a Silicon Valley context but hold little relevance for rural communities in Africa or South Asia, where access to affordable electricity is scarce.

Such hubs also often rely on a homogeneous talent pool, suffer from high living costs, deal with environmental sustainability concerns, are greatly affected by economic shifts and regulatory challenges, and in many ways face market saturation and fatigue.

Another important issue is evident in the recent decline of Silicon Valley's dominance as the premier innovation hub. This decline underscores the fragility of ecosystems if they are not actively nurtured. Rising living costs, a competitive global landscape, and the shift to remote work, which was greatly accelerated by COVID-19 and the pandemic years, have somewhat diminished the necessity of physical proximity to innovation hubs.

Regional hubs like Florida and Texas have recently emerged as attractive alternatives due to more affordable living costs and business-friendly environments. This highlights the importance of preserving and adapting an ecosystem's unique advantages, and a reminder that global ecosystems must also remain competitive. Without consistent effort to address evolving needs, such as affordability, even the largest, most prestigious ecosystems risk losing their edge to new, rising regions and players.

Local ecosystems complement global hubs by addressing regional challenges and fostering innovation tailored to specific contexts. Unlike global hubs, which often operate at a scale that overlooks localized needs, these provide agile solutions grounded in cultural, economic, and social realities, while offering a more diverse perspective.

For example, Israel offers a compelling case study of a local ecosystem driven by its unique military-to-civilian pipeline. Unit 8200 is an example of a military intelligence unit that has catalyzed advancements in various fields, including cybersecurity and AI, resulting in start-ups and solutions with global impact. Companies like Check Point and Waze emerged from this ecosystem. Check Point's Gil Shwed originally developed the idea in 8200, and his cofounders Marius Nacht and Shlomo Kramer formerly served there. With Waze, Ehud Shabtai, Amir Shinar, and Uri Levine all served in this elite unit, showcasing not only how military-originated innovation and training can shape civilian industries but how local ecosystems can make use of their unique aspects in a way that results in successful innovation and a more robust ecosystem.

Another notable example for the military-to-civilian pipeline that is unique to Israel, is Heka Global, which emerged from Unit 81. The company leveraged knowledge and experience gained in the defense and intelligence sectors. It successfully transitioned it into civilian applications, demonstrating how expertise from security-oriented units can drive innovation beyond military use.

Moreover, according to a report by Fusion,[34] entrepreneurs with backgrounds in Unit 8200 and other elite technological units in Israel tend to raise capital more easily thanks to the credibility, network, and technical reputation associated with their service. Similarly, serial entrepreneurs enjoy increased investor confidence, accelerating fundraising, and enhancing the likelihood of venture success.

Another interesting example, from a different field, is Konza Technopolis in Kenya, which has earned the nickname of "Silicon Savannah" and is well-known for developing fintech solutions such as M-Pesa, a mobile money transfer service that has revolutionized financial services

[34]Fusion VC, "The 2024 Pre-Seed Investment Landscape Report."

across Africa. This innovation was based on understanding the unique challenges faced by the unbanked population in the region.

These local hubs are, in many cases, though not all, cheaper to manage, provide additional resilience against economic downturns, and provide enhanced collaboration opportunities through connection with grassroot organizations.

Success Stories in Open Innovation: General Electric

Challenge: General Electric sought to tackle environmental challenges while maintaining industrial leadership.

Open Innovation Approach: Ecomagination focused on sustainability-driven crowdsourcing and partnerships with start-ups and researchers.

Outcome: The initiative was launched in 2005, and according to reports, by 2010, General Electric had exceeded every "Ecomagination" goal originally set, including $5 billion dedicated to clean-tech research and development, a 22 percent reduction in greenhouse gas emissions, a 30 percent reduction in facilities' water use, and a $130 million gain in energy efficiency savings.

Local ecosystems excel at building close-knit relationships between stakeholders, bringing together universities, government agencies, and businesses to foster education, technology, and job creation. Such ecosystems thrive on collaboration, as well as pooling limited resources to create a meaningful impact. However, they often face significant hurdles, including funding constraints, limited access to global research, and the persistent issue of brain drain as a result of immigration to global hubs.

At the same time, recent geopolitical shifts, such as trade tensions exemplified by the Trump tariffs, have created new opportunities for these ecosystems, especially in Europe, to attract talent migrating from the United States, showcasing how dynamic and fluid global innovation networks are. The tariff crisis, while a challenge, serves as a powerful catalyst for innovation, pushing local businesses and ecosystems to embrace open innovation, integrate start-up technologies like AI and blockchain, and reevaluate supply chains for efficiency. This environment accelerates the need for collaboration between start-ups, corporations, and governments to build resilience, optimize processes, and ultimately turn challenges into competitive advantages. For local hubs, this means not only surviving but thriving by leveraging these global shifts and fostering innovation-driven growth amid uncertainty.

Fragmentation is one of the most significant barriers to maximizing the potential of global and local ecosystems. Despite the interconnectedness offered by modern technology, ecosystems often operate in silos, limiting the flow of knowledge, resources, and collaboration. Differences in language, culture, and business practices can create communication barriers, while a lack of coordinated strategies can result in inefficient resource allocation.

In global ecosystems, fragmentation often occurs when corporations engage with multiple innovation hubs but fail to integrate their efforts effectively. This can lead to scattered investments, redundant initiatives, and an inability to adapt strategies to the unique dynamics of each region. Large multinational companies may also establish innovation activities in different countries but struggle to create synergy between them, reducing the overall impact of their efforts. In contrast, local ecosystems face a different type of fragmentation. **While they often foster strong relationships between local start-ups, academic institutions, and government agencies, they may lack the necessary infrastructure or global connections to scale their innovations beyond their immediate markets.**

Here, it is also essential to understand why vast differences in GDP persist globally between these hubs, despite the existence of a massive, connected global market. The eighteenth-century economist Adam Smith argued that specialization increases efficiency but that the extent of the market limits it. Today, the market is global, theoretically allowing for maximum specialization. However, not all the necessary inputs for production can be imported. A country's wealth resides in the diversity of its available capabilities, such as stable property rights, effective regulation, robust infrastructure, and specific, embedded labor skills.[35] These

[35]C. A. Hidalgo and R. Hausmann, "The Building Blocks of Economic Complexity," *Proceedings of the National Academy of Sciences* 106, no. 26 (2009): 10570–10575.

foundational capabilities must be developed locally, resulting in a gap between global and regional hubs, and between hubs of the same kind.

This is why, without strategic links to global ecosystems, local players risk becoming isolated, missing out on access to international expertise, funding, and expansion opportunities. Corporations engaging with multiple ecosystems may also spread their efforts too thinly, failing to adapt their strategies to the unique dynamics of each region. Similarly, local ecosystems may lack the infrastructure to connect effectively with global players, leaving them isolated from valuable opportunities for collaboration and growth. One highly effective solution is fostering knowledge-sharing agreements between corporations in different countries and in adjacent fields.

Meanwhile, to mitigate global fragmentation, corporations should actively integrate their various innovation hubs, ensuring that insights and resources flow seamlessly between different regions rather than operating as disconnected units. By leveraging partnerships across regions and industries, and improving integration between global and local ecosystems, companies can bridge fragmentation at both levels and access global expertise while ensuring that local innovations do not remain isolated. This approach enables innovation to transcend regional boundaries, address broader challenges, and provide added value.

A notable example of successful innovation activities by multinational organizations in a local ecosystem is Israel, where over 500 multinational corporations operate innovation hubs within the country. These companies offer us valuable lessons on how to innovate effectively, lessons that will be discussed in more detail later on. These companies innovate in Israel due to the country's density of start-ups, the relevance of the technologies being developed, and, of course, the growing maturity of the ecosystem.[36] In fact, Israel functions as a unique laboratory for open innovation, bridging multinational corporations and local start-ups. From this laboratory, many valuable lessons can be drawn that apply to innovation ecosystems worldwide. I have studied this innovation lab extensively over the years, gaining many insights that, when shared, can help others avoid costly mistakes.

[36]PwC Israel, "The State of Innovation. Operating Model Frameworks, Findings and Resources for Multinationals Innovating in Israel," April 2019.

While challenges persist, the opportunities for creating synergy between global and local ecosystems are immense. **Bridging the gap requires deliberate strategies and a commitment to open innovation.** This can be done successfully through:

1. Strategic Partnerships:
   One of the most effective ways to link global and local ecosystems is through partnerships. For example, through GE Healthcare, General Electric has collaborated with African health care providers to develop affordable medical devices and services tailored to local needs. Another good example is GE Healthcare's partnership with the Africa Medical Equipment Facility during the COVID-19 pandemic to support health care providers in Cameroon, Côte d'Ivoire, Kenya, Rwanda, Senegal, Tanzania, and Uganda, thereby providing further access to medical equipment. Such partnerships combine the scale and resources of global corporations with the contextual expertise of local stakeholders, creating impactful and scalable solutions.
2. Leveraging Innovation Intermediaries:
   Organizations such as Plug and Play, a leading venture capital firm operating in over 50 locations worldwide and an open innovation platform, can serve as innovation intermediaries, facilitating connections between global hubs and local ecosystems. These intermediaries help bridge gaps by coordinating efforts, promoting knowledge exchange, and fostering collaborative projects across geographies.
3. Digital Platforms for Collaboration:
   Technology has made it easier than ever for ecosystems to collaborate across borders. Platforms that have become everyday products, such as Zoom and WhatsApp, are enabling seamless communication. Many digital solutions enable virtual innovation events, online workshops, and facilitate networking and knowledge sharing. **What has become necessary during the COVID-19 pandemic, when many ecosystems transitioned to virtual collaborations, is now, years later, a common way of doing business.** This is an example of a crisis that lead to changes in patterns and behaviors, which persisted beyond the end of each crisis.

4. Government Initiatives:
   Policymakers play a crucial role in fostering collaboration between global and local ecosystems. Governments can incentivize multinational corporations to establish research and development centers in emerging markets or fund local start-ups to participate in international accelerator programs. A notable example is Israel's innovation policies, which include tax incentives and grants, that have successfully attracted global corporations while strengthening the local ecosystem. Israel provides tax credits to investors in Israeli start-up companies in the year the investment is made, when the shares are allocated to the investor by the company. Israel has also provided companies, such as Intel, with additional incentives, including grants and tax breaks, to attract global players to the country and expand their local operations. For example, Israel offers attractive tax incentives. While the corporate tax rate in Israel is 23 percent, qualifying organizations are entitled to reduced tax rates depending on their location and other conditions. A preferred technology enterprise operating in specific development areas may pay a corporate tax rate of just 5 percent.

Lessons Learned from Corporate Giants and Their Start-Up Collaborations: Pfizer and BioNTech

Before BioNTech became a household name due to its partnership with Pfizer on the COVID-19 vaccine, it was primarily a cancer research company specializing in mRNA-based immunotherapies.

Pfizer's collaboration with BioNTech began in 2018, focusing on developing mRNA-based influenza vaccines, and marked an early investment in mRNA technology. Pfizer's global infrastructure and vaccine research and development expertise were instrumental in advancing BioNTech's capabilities.

Lessons Learned:

1. Pfizer's partnership with BioNTech highlights the benefits of strategic collaborations in advancing innovative technologies like mRNA, allowing companies to leverage each other's strengths.

2. Pfizer's early investment in mRNA technology through its collaboration with BioNTech prepared the company for future breakthroughs.
3. The success of Pfizer and BioNTech's collaboration underscores the need for long-term commitment and patience, as many collaborations take years to yield tangible results. Still, they can lead to significant advancements in the field.

These policies reflect a broader strategic intent to position the country as a global innovation hub, fostering not just foreign investment but meaningful knowledge and technology transfer between ecosystems. In 2024, Israel launched a new national initiative to reshape its innovation landscape by establishing three new tech incubators, backed by up to €10 million each and additional direct start-up funding. This move aimed to nurture start-ups with significant global potential. The incubators are operated by selected investment bodies, including international and Israeli VCs and strategic corporate partners, and support start-ups from ideation to Series A. This is a bold step to strengthen Israel's competitiveness among global innovation hubs, diversify its start-up ecosystem, and position it as a world leader in complex, underinvested tech sectors.

Similarly, Israel has also doubled down on building a resilient FoodTech ecosystem, spearheaded by the Israel Innovation Authority. With strategic investment in both basic and applied research, Israel is advancing alternative protein technologies across the value chain, from early-stage R&D in academic labs to late-stage fermentation and commercialization. Government-backed incubators such as Tnuva's Fresh Start is now responsible for over a quarter of Israel's alt-protein start-ups. This proactive, long-term approach integrates public and private investments to drive breakthroughs, de-risk early innovation, and establish Israel as a global FoodTech powerhouse.

Beyond Israel, other countries are making significant strides in fostering innovation ecosystems. Saudi Arabia is rapidly emerging as a major AI hub, having launched its "GenAI for All" Initiative, which aims to support research, improve policies, and govern the use of generative AI. The country also plans to train one million citizens in AI as part of efforts to develop national capabilities in line with the goals of Saudi Vision 2030. Similarly, France has seen a remarkable surge in its innovation ecosystem, learning from Israel's model to boost start-up growth, attract international investment, and foster government-backed programs that support technological development.

A similar approach can be seen in Portugal, where the government has made a strategic decision to invest in the development of a TravelTech ecosystem. Portugal has strategically cultivated a TravelTech ecosystem by establishing "Startup Portugal" and "NEST—Tourism Innovation Center," a public–private anchor initiative of its Tourism 4.0 strategy. Portugal fosters digital innovation in tourism by aligning government policy, academia, corporations like Google and Microsoft, and start-up support systems. This integrated approach emphasizes entrepreneurship, tech adoption, pilot programs, and internationalization, allowing Portugal to create an attractive environment for start-ups and international investors.

Brazil has also embraced this model by establishing dedicated spaces where start-ups and corporations can collaborate under one roof. One notable example is Caldeira, located in Porto Alegre, which has become a dynamic hub for corporations and start-ups to connect, experiment, and collaborate on joint projects. Another key innovation hub in the country is Cubo Itaú in São Paulo, where start-ups and large enterprises work in proximity, enabling real-time exchange of ideas and fostering partnerships.

In addition, Amcham Brasil, the American Chamber of Commerce's presence in the country, is pivotal in connecting corporations with the start-up ecosystem, creating opportunities for collaboration, innovation, and business development. Their initiatives bring together industry leaders, entrepreneurs, innovators, and consultants, to bridge the gap between corporate needs and start-up-driven solutions.

During a recent visit to Brazil, I also encountered an inspiring model where entrepreneurs and corporations were brought together within the university campus. This initiative demonstrates how academic institutions can serve as bridges between cutting-edge research, entrepreneurial ventures, and corporate innovation needs. By facilitating such interactions, universities help accelerate the commercialization of new ideas and create stronger connections between industry and academia.

Further examples include Shenzhen's transformation into a global innovation hub, which was driven in many ways by government investments. Estonia's e-governance ecosystem has successfully leveraged digital-first policies to attract international attention and talent, making it a global leader in public-sector innovation.

As discussed, these examples highlight the importance of aligning local strengths with global ambitions. The relationship between global and local innovation ecosystems is not a zero-sum game. Instead, it represents a dynamic where each can amplify the strengths of the other through intensive collaboration among players across different levels.[37]

By building bridges through strategic partnerships and leveraging the skill sets of the right intermediaries, stakeholders can create resilient networks that integrate the best of both worlds. In doing so, they unlock the full potential of open innovation, ensuring that they enjoy and benefit from technological advancements.

Ultimately, successfully navigating this interplay will define the future for all ecosystem participants, setting some players, whether governments, corporations, or start-ups, ahead of their respective competition, while others will lag behind or even disappear altogether.

[37]K. Oksanen and A. Hautamäki, "Sustainable Innovation: A Competitive Advantage for Innovation Ecosystems," *Technology Innovation Management Review* 5, no. 10 (2015): 24–30.

CHAPTER 7

Where Smart People Are: Leveraging External Talent

No one has a monopoly on knowledge the way that, say, IBM had in the 1960s in computing, or that Bell Labs had through the 1970s in communications. When useful knowledge exists in companies of all sizes and also in universities, non-profits and individual minds, it makes sense to orient your innovation efforts to accessing, building upon and integrating that external knowledge into useful products and services.

—Professor Henry Chesbrough

As mentioned above, Joy's law, coined by Sun Microsystems cofounder Bill Joy, states that **the majority of the smartest people will always work for someone else**. This might initially seem discouraging for organizations hoping to innovate; however, in truth, this is not a barrier; instead, it is an opportunity.

This idea serves as the cornerstone of open innovation. Organizations must recognize that the solutions to their most pressing challenges likely lie outside their walls but still within their reach. **Start-ups, representing an unparalleled force in driving innovation, operate with an agility that corporations struggle to replicate**, and often attract unique talents and grow human capital with distinct capabilities that larger organizations tend to lack.

These smaller, more agile players thrive on risk and creativity, unencumbered by the many layers of bureaucracy that slow down corporate decision making. They specialize in disruptive ideas that challenge the status quo, bringing fresh perspectives and often bold solutions to the table. If you are a corporate leader and these remarks make you to protest, I am glad, for this means I was able to create the necessary "shock" that might deliver change. If you agree, you will soon gain access to a more practical guidebook for innovation. Organizations can leverage the advantages of such players by establishing partnerships with start-ups through various mechanisms. **The comprehensive list below is meant to help you choose what kind of mechanism will fit you best:**

- *Corporate Accelerators and Incubators:* Accelerators and incubators are programs that help start-ups grow, the first focusing on helping existing start-ups grow in scale, with the latter assisting start-ups in their early stages to build their business models and launch their products and services. Such programs create environments where start-ups can collaborate with established companies, providing them with resources, mentorship, and access to market opportunities, as well as concrete industry challenges to address. This allows corporations to gain insight into emerging technologies and business models. Mercedes-Benz, for example, utilizes the Startup Autobahn, in collaboration with Plug and Play, to gain access to game-changing technology and facilitate collaboration between start-ups and Mercedes-Benz, combining specific technological expertise with comprehensive automotive expertise. The company claims that this program enables it to determine within a short period whether it can collaborate with start-ups and form partnerships.
- *Pilot and Integration Programs:* Corporations can run pilot and integration programs with start-ups to test new products or services in a controlled environment. This approach allows companies to assess the feasibility of innovations before implementing them at a full scale. It is worth noting that the optimal stage for corporate investment in start-ups typically begins immediately after a successful pilot program. Pilots are the most effective indicator of success and due diligence, offering corporations direct exposure to the start-up's technology, team, and scalability potential, insights that venture capital funds can only approximate. This unique vantage point allows corporations to identify and capitalize on high-potential opportunities. The most natural evolution of open innovation involves transitioning from conducting pilots

and implementations to actively investing in start-ups that have proven their value to the corporation through previously successful collaborations. For example, a leading insurance company in Israel, and a client of mine, had leveraged several pilot successes as a stepping stone for strategic investments, reinforcing its innovation strategy while fostering long-term partnerships and value for stakeholders. Some of these investments proved to be a true source of value creation, resulting in millions of dollars in efficiency gains, and adding millions in equity earnings. In my experience with my clients, when done correctly, and when the corporation is fully engaged, from top management down to the operational teams, the conversion ratio I achieve from pilot to integration is 70 percent, far higher than the 30 percent reported as the average in industry studies. This significant difference stems from the level of engagement: When a corporation is truly committed, strategically, culturally, and operationally, the chances of scaling a pilot successfully increase dramatically. We will discuss engagement in detail further on.

- *Commercialization Program*: This effective and hybrid approach combines elements of accelerators and pilot programs. Unlike traditional accelerators, which focus on mentoring and networking, these take a more hands-on approach by actively codeveloping start-ups with corporate partners. One standout example is the Builders program, which pioneered this category and coined the term commercialization program, a leading initiative partnering with prominent Fortune 100 companies such as Coca-Cola, Turner, Walmart, Maersk, and Mercedes-Benz, which combines structured corporate involvement with the agility of start-ups, enabling the rapid development and market validation of new solutions. The main reason this model works so well is that it combines building the internal methodology inside the large organizations to support the adoption of new technologies and the support of senior leadership from the corporations, seeing Walmart or Coca-Cola's CEO taking part in program events or thought process was a common sight and the thoughtful connection to real business problems that matter and have an impact on the organization as well as a budget attached to solve them, helped make sure the innovation is focused on commercialization. This direct business alignment motivates their employees to collaborate and significantly increases the program's success rate. The Builders' model is also particularly effective because it aligns corporate needs with start-up innovation, ensuring both sides gain strategic value.

- *Venture Clienting*: In this model, large firms become early customers of start-ups, integrating innovative products or services into their operations without significant equity stakes. This allows corporations to test new technologies while providing start-ups with valuable feedback and real-world application opportunities. This model stands in contrast to outdated corporate approaches that demand equity in exchange for pilot opportunities, an attitude that often backfires. In one notable case, I consulted a manufacturing company and was told by their CEO in our first meeting that he recently insisted on receiving 25 percent equity in a start-up merely for agreeing to pilot their IoT solution. The start-up refused and instead partnered with a competitor. Within three months, the competitor had a market-ready solution, while the original corporation chose to develop in-house, spending three years and $5 million, only to arrive late to market with a significantly inferior product.
- *Innovation Challenges and Hackathons*: Corporations can host competitions that invite start-ups to propose solutions to specific problems. Companies like GE utilize open innovation challenges to gather ideas from start-ups and entrepreneurs. These competitions foster creativity while helping corporations identify potential partners who can contribute innovative solutions to pressing industry challenges. One example is GE HealthCare India, where the company claims "the brightest minds converge to redefine healthcare." External innovation challenges, combining corporate employees with external participants such as entrepreneurs, students, and researchers, tend to be more effective than internal-only initiatives, as they promote cross-pollination of ideas and expose the corporation to diverse perspectives and talent.

- *Corporate Venture Capital*: Corporations can invest in start-ups through their CVC arms. This provides financial support to start-ups and enables corporations to gain insights into new technologies and business models, potentially leading to a quick go-to-market strategy. For example, Intel Capital has invested in numerous tech start-ups to enhance its innovation pipeline. It states that it identifies and invests in disruptive start-ups that push boundaries in their respective areas of work, including AI, data analytics, autonomous systems, and semiconductor innovation. This allows the company to navigate its challenges and improve long-term growth. Some examples of its investments include Anodot, Astera Labs, Axonne, Hypersonix, KFBIO, Lilt, MemVerge, ProPlus Electronics, Retrace, Spectrum Materials, and Xsight Labs. Another good example is Amadeus Ventures, the CVC arm of Amadeus, which began its journey with strategic investments in start-ups and has since expanded its activities to include pilot programs aimed at integrating and commercializing innovative technologies to strengthen Amadeus's portfolio and accelerate the adoption of cutting-edge solutions within the travel and hospitality industries. In other cases, corporations are the leading partners in independently managed funds, and one example is the global insurance company MAPFRE, which is the senior investor in Alma Mundi Ventures, a VC fund focused on insurtech and healthtech.

Academic institutions further expand the horizons of open innovation. Universities and research centers provide not only groundbreaking research but also access to a steady pipeline of highly skilled talent. Such partnerships bridge theoretical research and practical applications, allowing corporations to harness the academic world's intellectual capital to tackle real-world challenges. Here are some of the ways that organizations can access their insights and value:

- Collaborative Research Projects: Corporations can engage in joint research initiatives that align with their strategic goals. Such partnerships enable companies to leverage academic expertise while addressing specific challenges. For instance, Siemens collaborates with various universities through its Centers of Knowledge Interchange program, first introduced in 1999, to drive innovation in engineering. The partnership is based on the sponsored university's core values and working concepts. Each office serves as an interface between the industrial and academic worlds, with a responsibility to align Siemens's industrial perspectives and needs with the academic and research resources of the university and create opportunities for research collaborations. These offices act as a liaison between the two parties; the universities and Siemens.

- Technology Transfer Offices: These units facilitate the commercialization of research taking place in universities, while often acting as a channel between academia and the business world. These offices have become increasingly popular, both in the United States, where this trend originated, and in many other countries, such as Japan, China, Israel, and European countries. Copaxone, for example, the first and only non-interferon agent for the treatment of relapsing–remitting multiple sclerosis, was patented by Yeda Research and Development Company, the commercial arm of the Weizmann Institute of Science, and licensed to Teva Pharmaceuticals.
- Internship and Co-op Programs: By offering internships or cooperative education programs, companies can engage students in real-world projects while simultaneously evaluating potential future employees. This approach fosters a talent pipeline directly aligned with corporate needs. Professor Gil Avnimelech, for example, leads such a program at the Faculty of Business Administration, Ono Academic College. Likewise, Dr. Yossi Maaravi leads a similar notable program at the Adelson School of Entrepreneurship at the Interdisciplinary Center in Herzliya.
- Innovation Hubs: Initiatives like the University of Cincinnati's 1819 Innovation Hub, founded in 2018 in honor of the University's visionaries who founded the university in 1819, at the Center for the Silicon Heartland, exemplify how universities can create physical spaces that foster collaboration between students, faculty,

and industry leaders. These hubs facilitate interdisciplinary approaches to problem-solving, enabling companies to connect with researchers with relevant expertise. These allow organizations to collaborate with inventors from early conceptualization through to commercialization. This specific program claims that over 100 products already in the market were developed there.

- Industry Advisory Boards: Corporations can establish advisory boards composed of university faculty and researchers to guide their R&D strategies. These boards offer insights into emerging trends and technologies that are relevant to the industry.
- Joint Degree Programs and Talent Development Programs: Collaborating on educational programs allows companies to influence curriculum development in ways that align with industry needs. For example, IBM has partnered with universities to create specialized degree programs in data science, including at Carleton University, where the program aims to enhance Carleton's Institute for Data Science and equip students with the skills needed for the job market, such as those in demand at IBM. In some cases, corporations sponsor specific university courses in exchange for students working on final projects that directly address the corporation's real-world challenges. By aligning educational programs with industry needs, businesses can ensure a steady flow of talent equipped with the skills necessary for today's dynamic work environment.

Independent innovators, such as freelancers, consultants, or researchers, can also offer unique insights and specialized knowledge that can be invaluable for organizations. These can gain value, through:

- Consulting Arrangements: Engaging independent experts on a project basis allows companies to access specialized skills without the long-term commitment of hiring full-time employees. This flexibility enables organizations to adapt quickly to changing project requirements.
- Crowdsourcing Ideas: Platforms that facilitate crowdsourcing allow corporations to gather diverse ideas from a wide range of

contributors. This method enhances creativity while democratizing the innovation process by inviting input from various stakeholders.

Finally, collaboration among corporations is another crucial aspect of open innovation. Companies can pool resources and expertise by partnering with other organizations, whether they are competitors or other businesses, primarily technological partners. This can be done through:

- Strategic Alliances: Companies often form strategic alliances to combine their strengths in specific areas. An example is the partnership between BMW and Toyota on hydrogen fuel cell technology, announced in 2024, which enables both companies to share research and development costs while advancing sustainable automotive solutions.
- Joint Ventures: Joint ventures enable two or more companies to collaborate on a specific project while sharing risks and rewards. The collaboration between Sony and Ericsson in mobile technology from 2001 to 2012 exemplifies how joint ventures can leverage complementary strengths for mutual benefit.
- Industry Collaboratives: Corporations may join industry-specific collaborations focusing on shared challenges. The "Open Invention Network" is an example where various technology companies collaborate on patent protection for Linux-related technologies. The community comprises over 4,000 members who collectively own more than 3 million patents and applications. Some of its Members include Alphabet, Microsoft, IBM, Red Hat, Sony, Phillips, the Royal Bank of Canada, Meta, and many other partners across industries and around the world.
- Cocreation Initiatives: Companies like LEGO have embraced co-creation by inviting other businesses and customers to participate in product development processes through platforms like LEGO Ideas, a platform where fans submit and vote on new product ideas, with winning designs commercialized, and creators receiving a share of the revenue. This collaborative approach generates innovative product concepts while fostering community engagement.

- Cross-Industry Collaborations: Collaborating across different industries can lead to unique innovations by combining diverse expertise. For instance, health care companies might partner with tech firms to develop digital health solutions, integrating medical knowledge with technological advancements.

Building robust networks is essential for corporations aiming to capitalize on external talent. Successful open innovation requires more than isolated partnerships; it demands interconnected ecosystems where knowledge, resources, and expertise flow freely. These thrive on relationships cultivated not only with a partner but across the ecosystem.

While it is crucial to leverage external talent in today's business environment, the journey toward effective open innovation is not without its challenges. Organizations often encounter resistance to change within their ranks, stemming from fears of intellectual property loss, misaligned objectives, or cultural differences between external partners and internal teams.

CHAPTER 8

Build, Buy, or Partner—Deciding on the Right Approach

Before asking for more Headcount and resources, teams must demonstrate why they cannot get what they want done using AI.

—Tobi Lütke

As organizations strive to stay competitive, they face a strategic decision: should they build new ventures internally, make minority investments, acquire proven start-ups, or partner with others to cocreate value?

These decisions are crucial for businesses exploring new opportunities, testing disruptive models, or seeking to scale their ventures. Moreover, **in a world where the pace of change is only accelerating and competitors are not standing still, these choices are not only about growth and innovation but about sheer survival**.

In fact, as a result of the vast disruptions experienced across industries in recent years, and further disruptions expected, I believe that it is a question that almost all organizations are currently facing. Each of these strategic options has its advantages, challenges, and ideal contexts, and organizations must learn how to make the right choice for them in each case:

1. Build Internally

Building internally means launching and executing new ventures using corporate resources, talent, and capabilities. The key advantages are full control, preserving 100 percent ownership, and leveraging the company's infrastructure, customer base, and data. This can help mitigate some inherent risks associated with launching a new business or product.

Success Stories in Open Innovation: Peugeot Citroën

Challenge: Peugeot Citroën needed to develop next-gen automotive technology while reducing costs.

Open Innovation Approach: OpenLabs, a network of research partnerships with universities and institutions, fosters scientific collaboration.

Outcome: The initiative has helped Peugeot Citroën advance electric vehicle technology and smart mobility solutions.

However, building internally has significant challenges. Time to success is generally much longer compared to start-up environments. Despite more available resources, large organizations often find that their ventures take longer and cost significantly more compared to start-ups, which can develop and bring solutions to market quickly and efficiently.

This course of action is best suited for corporations with a significant market share that are looking to build new products within their existing business structure, while having the runway to experiment, with a preference for low levels of uncertainty. It is best used when there are no available partners or existing solutions, and when there are minimal time constraints. This option is therefore not relevant in most cases when dealing with disruptive technology. It is worth noting that time to market is the most critical resource companies have in these cases, and that customers and competitors alike will not wait. In-house teams often lack entrepreneurial experience, and integrating new ventures into existing corporate governance frameworks typically results in slower execution. This frequently creates unnecessary delays and sometimes maintains failing ideas longer than they would have in a start-up with limited resources.

A start-up has another advantage here, in the form of specialization. A corporation focuses on many things, with technology being just one of them. Therefore, a start-up has a deeper understanding and specialization in its field of expertise, enabling it to successfully execute innovative visions more quickly (Figure 8.1).

Based on my experience, relying on in-house efforts should only be done in rare cases, where a corporation will benefit more than lose, and when absolutely necessary. In the vast majority of situations, there is an alternative,

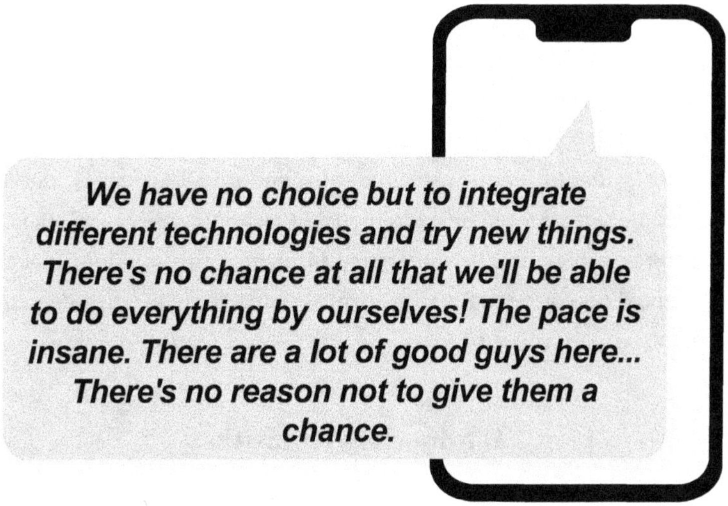

Figure 8.1 Leadership perspective: The urgency of integrating new technologies

and open innovation offers an agile and efficient path based on leveraging external expertise and resources instead of the typically slow and expensive internal processes. Companies cannot afford a slow time to market in such a time of increasingly rapid change, and searching for solutions outside the organization should be the default in most cases. This does not mean that there is no room for internal innovation, but this should be done only when there are good reasons for it. In my experience, investment in internal innovation should require approval from the CEO, and only happen when he has made sure that there are no better alternatives, similar to Shopify's CEO Tobi Lütke's famous quote that teams must demonstrate why AI can't perform a job before they are permitted to ask for more headcount and resources. Over the course of my 25 years of experience, I have met many vice presidents who pushed for internal innovation solely because of internal politics and ego, rather than in cases where it was truly needed. It is up to CEOs to ensure that internal politics do not cost their organizations both money and time.

2. Buy

Acquisitions involve a corporation absorbing an existing start-up or a proven business, offering full control post-acquisition to integrate the new venture into the corporate structure. Mergers and acquisitions are known for their high failure rate of 60 to 90 percent.[38] The majority of which do not deliver the expected outcomes, and success very much depends on cultural integration, leadership alignment, and postacquisition strategy.

This course of action is suitable when an idea already exists, the corporation needs a proven business model or technology to complement its existing portfolio, and it is interested in owning this solution. It is also best suited for corporations with adequate capabilities for the integration process.

3. Minority Acquisition

Minority acquisitions involve a corporate entity investing in a start-up, acquiring a stake of less than 50 percent in equity, typically 20 to 30 percent, and often 10 percent or less, depending on the sector.[39] This option offers lower capital commitment than acquisitions and gives the company a "foot in the door" in interesting fields.

However, based on my experience, such investments should ideally follow a successful pilot. A pilot dramatically reduces the risk of investment, as it demonstrates the start-up's ability to deliver tangible results that are relevant to the corporate challenges. Without this critical step, equity investments are often limited to mere exposure. Following such a pilot, even in a minority position, corporate investors can influence the start-up's roadmap and strategic direction, while gaining exposure to cutting-edge technologies and emerging markets through the start-up's activity.

A successful pilot demonstrates the start-up's ability to deliver tangible results, making the investment both strategic and impactful. For example, the investment fund of a leading Israeli insurance company, Menora Mivtachim, specializes in investing in start-ups, primarily after successful

---

[38]M. Apaydin, "Optimizing Implementation Schedules for a Successful Post-Merger Integration (PMI): A Behavioral View," *Journal of Business Strategy* 46, no. 1–2 (2025): 11–28.

[39]P. P. Ouimet, "What Motivates Minority Acquisitions? The Trade-Offs Between a Partial Equity Stake and Complete Integration," *The Review of Financial Studies* 26, no. 4 (2013): 1021–1047.

pilots, to ensure alignment with its strategic goals and, most importantly, solve corporate pain points. An example of how the company invests following a demonstration of value is the company's investment in the AI fintech DigitalOwl. In 2018, the start-up initially approached Menora Mivtachim with a solution for summarizing legal documents using AI. However, following a meeting with the insurer, the start-up shifted focus to summarizing medical records. A pilot was launched within 72 hours of that meeting and quickly demonstrated the technology's value. As a result, Menora Mivtachim invested in the company's seed round, which was later translated into significant equity gains as the start-up reached its full potential. Notably, one of DigitalOwl's co-early investors is the famous Prof. Amnon Shashua. Being a minor investor may carry additional risks without this extra step, and its return on investment (ROI) is often unpredictable. Many corporations struggle to achieve substantial returns, with some even lacking control over the start-up's direction. Pilots serve as an effective tool for managing and mitigating these risks. Pilots between a corporate and a start-up are the best due diligence one can imagine.

This course of action suits companies seeking exposure to new technologies or business models without assuming full control. It is often considered a lower-risk approach, but with the trade-off of limited influence on the investment outcome.

Some challenges here include difficulty measuring key performance indicators (KPIs) and uncertainty regarding long-term business benefits. Lack of full control is another problem, but corporations can still influence start-ups to ensure they align with their strategic goals and deliver tangible returns.

4. Partner

As mentioned earlier, partnering with external organizations has become increasingly popular in recent years, providing a significantly faster and more efficient route to market than any other alternative. From my personal experience working with many leading organizations around the world, I have found that pilots are the best way to kickstart a partnership and relationship with a start-up, achieving maximum impact and speed to market.

This model has a higher success rate than building internally, and significantly lower inherent risks, allowing organizations to speed up the journey to profitability.

Some challenges here include difficulties in aligning the corporation with the partner. Another major pitfall is bureaucracy, as corporate structures can stifle creativity, slow decision making, and hinder innovation.

This model is suited for companies looking to enter new, adjacent markets, adopt new business models with the support of experienced entrepreneurs who can scale ventures rapidly, offer new products, improve existing products and methods based on disruptive technology, and stay ahead of technological advancements. This approach is also ideal for companies wishing to minimize risks while leveraging external talent and innovation.

When considering which path to take for new business ventures, organizations must weigh the costs, timeframes, and level of control each option requires. Building internally offers complete control, but it comes at a high price and requires significant time. Minority investments are lower risk financially but provide limited control and often unclear returns. Acquiring a start-up offers control but often leads to integration difficulties and cultural clashes.

According to Vantage Partners,[40] the decision depends on several conditions, such as the strategic importance of the initiative, the risks of working externally, existing capability gaps, time-to-market pressures, and the volatility of the product environment. Internal "build" approaches are most suitable when the strategic impact is high, existing market capabilities are low, and organizations have sufficient time and resources to develop solutions themselves. "Buy" strategies are more appropriate when capabilities already exist in the market, the need for integration is manageable, and the organization requires faster time to market than internal development allows. "Invest" strategies are often employed when capabilities are emerging but still uncertain, allowing firms to make strategic bets with a moderate level of commitment. "Ally," or partner strategies become the best choice when organizations must move quickly, need to

[40]Vantage Partners, "Build, Buy, Invest, Partner: Strategic Options for Growth."

coordinate across multiple players, or seek to share risks and resources with external experts.

Compared to the rest of the other alternatives, **partnering, which is the basis of open innovation, offers a balanced and efficient approach.** This route minimizes risks while allowing organizations to tap into external expertise and accelerate time to market while maintaining flexibility. By cocreating value with external innovators, businesses can leverage diverse perspectives, access cutting-edge technologies, and quickly adapt to market changes. Ultimately, **open innovation and partnerships present the most promising path forward, enabling organizations to innovate effectively without incurring the full burden of internal development or requiring costly acquisitions.**

It is worth noting here that open innovation fundamentally challenges traditional R&D and IT structures within organizations. Instead of assuming that internal teams must always build or develop solutions from scratch, open innovation introduces an alternative: finding, testing, and integrating external solutions that may be faster, cheaper, or more advanced. This shift creates a healthy competitive dynamic, where internal and external innovation paths are evaluated side by side, encouraging better decision making. In April 2025, as previously mentioned, Shopify CEO Tobi Lütke informed employees that no new hires would be made unless they could demonstrate that AI could not perform the job. In some ways, this is similar, and employees should only be hired if there is no relevant external solution available. In every opportunity, organizations should, therefore, ask themselves: *Should we build this internally, or is there a smarter, faster, more cost-effective solution outside?*

By understanding the advantages and pitfalls of each option, companies can make informed decisions, ensuring their ventures are positioned for long-term success in a rapidly evolving business landscape.

CHAPTER 9

Balancing Open Innovation with In-House R&D

Open is key to innovation.

—Arvind Krishna

In the quest for sustainable innovation, navigating the delicate balance between leveraging external partnerships and nurturing in-house research and development is a challenging task. While open innovation provides access to external talent, technologies, and ideas, internal R&D remains a critical engine for building core competencies and maintaining control while protecting intellectual property. This is particularly important in more technologically intense industries.[41] Successfully integrating these two approaches is not merely a strategic choice; it is a necessity for organizations aiming to lead.

Organizations can effectively balance the two by adopting a strategic approach that recognizes the complementary roles of both processes, as the interplay between these two models of innovation allows companies to capitalize on the best of both worlds. While a high level of internal R&D is not necessarily associated with high levels of product-based innovation, a positive relationship between internal R&D and new product partnership still exists. In many ways, **in-house capabilities provide the foundational knowledge necessary to effectively absorb and integrate external innovations**. Successfully balancing open innovation with in-house R&D requires deliberate strategies to create synergy and minimize conflict. Organizations must develop dynamic capabilities that enable

[41]F. D. O. Paula and J. F. D. Silva, "Balancing Internal and External R&D Strategies to Improve Innovation and Financial Performance," *BAR-Brazilian Administration Review* 15, no. 2 (2018): e170129.

them to adaptively manage both internal and external knowledge flows, including an organizational culture that encourages collaboration, learning, and flexibility in integrating new ideas from various sources.

Crucially, organizations must allocate dedicated development resources and time for open innovation. **Without structured internal support, including staffing, budget, and dedicated work hours, external collaborations will struggle to deliver impact.** This means that the organization must treat open innovation with at least the same seriousness and operational rigor as internal R&D efforts.

Actions that must be taken include:

1. Establishing Clear Roles: Organizations should define the distinct but complementary roles of internal R&D teams and external innovation partners. For instance, internal teams can focus on refining and scaling current solutions, or on facilitating work with external partners, while external collaborations explore uncharted territories and disruptive technologies. Moreover, before developing anything internally, organizations should always examine whether a similar solution already exists externally. Only if no suitable option is available should they proceed with internal development. This constant comparison of alternatives must consider not only cost but, above all, time to market.
2. Creating Cross-Functional Teams: Integrated teams comprising different stakeholders within the organization, with the help of external collaborators, can bridge the gap between the two models. These teams facilitate knowledge transfer, align goals, and integrate externally developed solutions seamlessly.
3. Investing in Governance Frameworks: Effective governance is crucial for managing external partnerships and ensuring alignment with internal objectives, including setting clear agreements on intellectual property, well-defined project timelines, and KPIs.
4. Allocating Dedicated Resources: Organizations must designate specific budgets, staff, and protected time for open innovation initiatives. Treating open innovation as a core strategic priority, not an extracurricular activity will ensure long-term commitment and operational success.

5. Building Internal Infrastructure to Support Collaboration: Establishing systems, tools, and operational processes that enable efficient external engagement, such as collaboration platforms, innovation onboarding procedures, and streamlined legal review processes, will reduce friction and accelerate the integration of external solutions. Equally important, IT and development teams must allocate dedicated time and personnel to support the evaluation and integration of external technological solutions, ensuring these efforts are prioritized and resourced adequately.

Success Stories in Open Innovation: NASA

Challenge: NASA faced technological and budget constraints in space exploration.

Open Innovation Approach: Through the NASA Tournament Lab, the agency crowdsources solutions to aerospace challenges and partners with private firms, such as SpaceX.

Outcome: Open innovation has led to advancements in areas such as astronaut gear, robotic systems, and reusable rocket technology.

While integrating open innovation and in-house R&D offers immense potential, it is not without challenges. Resistance to change is a common barrier, as internal teams may perceive external collaborations as a threat to their autonomy or relevance. Building a culture that values collaboration and views external partners as allies rather than competitors is key to overcoming such resistance.

IBM's transformation in recent years provides one of the clearest examples of how cultural change is essential to balancing open innovation with traditional R&D. When IBM acquired Red Hat, the move was not only because it was a leader in open-source software but also because it was an "Open Organization,"[42] with a culture that emphasized transparency, meritocracy, and community-driven innovation, values often at

[42] J. Whitehurst, *The Open Organization: Igniting Passion and Performance* (Harvard Business Press, 2015).

odds with IBM's historically proprietary R&D culture. Integrating Red Hat required IBM to rethink how success was measured: Instead of focusing on patent counts and IP ownership, IBM began to evaluate contributions to open-source ecosystems, code-sharing velocity, and community impact, resulting in a more agile R&D structure. In essence, IBM's open innovation journey demonstrates that achieving balance is not merely structural but also cultural.

Luckily, as the demand for rapid innovation grows, many R&D departments are learning from such cases and are shifting their focus. Instead of simply expanding their in-house development teams, they are increasing the number of project managers and product teams responsible for integrating start-up technologies. This trend is expected to continue, reshaping the R&D departments of the future for many years to come.

Success Stories in Open Innovation: IBM

Challenge: IBM, traditionally known for a proprietary, patent-focused R&D culture, needed to pivot toward an open, cloud-centric ecosystem.

Open Innovation Approach: IBM acquired Red Hat for $34 billion, not only for its technology but for its deep open-source culture and philosophy of collaboration, transparency, and community.

Outcome: The acquisition facilitated a fundamental shift in IBM's internal R&D metrics, moving from counting patents and proprietary IP to measuring contributions to external open-source communities and overall ecosystem strength, effectively integrating an external culture to achieve agility in a way that resulted in the ability to foster greater innovation and community engagement.

Another challenge lies in aligning timelines and expectations. Startups, for example, often operate with shorter innovation cycles, while corporate R&D teams may prioritize long-term goals. **To address this, corporations must adopt flexible processes that accommodate the differing paces of innovation, as well as clear KPIs that will assist them in measuring the value of each project.** The future of R&D leadership will very much depend on fostering a culture that values flexibility and external collaboration, and the most successful innovation teams will be led by individuals who prioritize results over hierarchy. **This requires leadership to be driven not by ego but by impact**, which should be measured not by how many employees they manage but by the number of successful projects executed in collaboration with external partners and their impact.

Organizations operating in highly technological fields or fields with intense start-up activity and disruption potential must invest conjointly in both internal and external R&D regardless of their goals. In contrast, low-tech organizations can focus on one or the other in the short term, but even for them, this will not be enough, and they will have to find the right balance in the future.[43] This approach allows corporations to harness the full spectrum of possibilities while enjoying both worlds.

[43]Paula and Silva, "Balancing Internal and External R&D Strategies," e170129.

CHAPTER 10

The Role of Strategic Consultancies

What is the calculus of innovation? The calculus of innovation is really quite simple: Knowledge drives innovation, innovation drives productivity, productivity drives economic growth.

—Dr. William R. Brody

Strategic consultancies and management firms are valuable resources for corporations seeking to refine their strategies, enhance operational efficiency, and navigate complex market landscapes. They bring much-needed expertise and knowledge; however, when it comes to innovation, **strategic consultancies, often considered the go-to solution for fresh ideas and strategic direction, face significant limitations.**

The generic frameworks, standardized playbooks, and "cookie-cutter" methodologies used by these firms can provide structure but often fail to address nuanced challenges related to fostering innovation. While their structured methodologies can provide clarity, they often lack the agility needed to fully keep pace with fast-moving innovation landscapes. In the world of innovation, this approach is more likely than not to fail to align with their clients' unique culture, processes, and the market conditions needed to implement open innovation, while resulting in recommendations that, though well intentioned, remain too generic to drive meaningful innovation.

The key limitation of strategic consultancies lies not in their overall value, which is considerable, but in their limited ability to recognize emerging innovation opportunities in real time. While they can provide valuable insights into market trends and best practices, **a good corporate innovation leader will always have an advantage in understanding emerging opportunities. Why? Because they have direct access to**

early-stage entrepreneurs operating under the radar, before they become visible start-ups. This early exposure enables internal innovation teams to identify trends when they are still just ideas, providing them with a meaningful strategic advantage.

That said, it is essential to note that consultancies can still play a crucial role in the broader innovation ecosystem. Consultancies should position themselves as facilitators and enablers of open innovation, assisting organizations in harnessing external ideas while fostering a culture conducive to innovation as part of a broader innovation ecosystem.

Where such consultancy firms can truly shine is in their ability to bridge gaps and connect different members of the ecosystem, introducing corporations to relevant start-ups and other beneficial partners. Instead of dictating solutions, they can curate relationships, facilitate pilots, and help organizations navigate the process of external innovation.

Consultancies can also introduce new technologies to organizations, exposing them to solutions to their challenges, assist in establishing different evolution metrics to support innovation endeavors, and work with organizations to promote the much-needed shift in organizational mindsets, away from entrenched and risk-averse hierarchies and cultures, and toward the open mindset that is required to truly succeed in innovating. The latter can be achieved through workshops, lectures, training sessions, and various leadership programs tailored for board members and managers at different levels.

In conclusion, traditional strategic consultancies bring significant value to the ecosystem, but **they are not equipped to serve as the primary drivers of innovation and discovery**. While they may lack the agility, familiarity, and creative depth needed to directly drive innovation, their value lies in their ability to indirectly enable and support it, serving as valuable allies who offer connections, tools, and frameworks. By embracing this evolved role, strategic consultancies will continue to serve as trusted partners.

PART 2

The Practice

CHAPTER 11

Building a Corporate Culture That Welcomes Collaboration

No matter how brilliant your mind or strategy, if you're playing a solo game, you'll always lose out to a team.

—Reid Hoffman

Innovation thrives in collaboration, and to successfully collaborate with the right partners, **organizations must position themselves as a desirable partner within their ecosystem**, attracting the right start-ups, academic institutions, and other key players.

This requires more than just understanding that the organization must innovate; it requires organizations to realize how to proactively attract partners and create an environment where such partnerships can flourish.

This requires, first and foremost, cultivating a corporate culture that prioritizes openness, agility, and collaborative thinking, with the understanding that organizational culture is the beating heart of any organization, dictating how employees think, act, and interact with one another, as well as with members of the ecosystem.

Cultivating the right culture is the first crucial step for corporations aiming to become attractive partners and successfully innovate through open innovation.

In the past, rigid and hierarchical cultures were the common standard for many organizations. They successfully delivered the expected results. However, today, when organizations fail to keep pace with the competition and technological advancements, such an approach is a recipe for stagnation. **Organizations will innovate or die in the future, and this process begins with creating the right mindset today.**

As I often say in my lectures, companies need a cultural shift toward openness, agility, collaboration, and a relentless pursuit of external innovation to succeed in today's fast-paced world. A culture of innovation and curiosity is the only way to stay relevant, allowing companies to adapt and update their businesses in response to market changes in real time.

As Jim Whitehurst[44] emphasizes, true cultural transformation happens when leadership no longer views control as strength but rather sees empowerment, transparency, meritocracy, participation, and shared purpose as the foundation of success. Likewise, Lou Gerstner, who transformed IBM's bureaucratic giant into an adaptive, customer-focused organization, put it simply by saying that culture is not just part of the game but that it is the game.[45] Both leaders underscore that collaboration cannot be mandated; it must be lived, modeled, and rewarded.

To do so, organizations should begin by challenging and dismantling silos. Departments often operate as independent entities, focusing narrowly on their objectives with little consideration for the broader organizational goals or external opportunities, limiting the potential for cross-pollination of ideas. **Companies should, instead, create cross-functional teams, where members from different departments come together to solve specific problems and pursue innovation projects.**

Above all, leadership plays a pivotal role in shaping corporate culture. As Gerstner proved at IBM, cultural change begins at the top and succeeds only when leaders embody and reinforce the desired values on a daily basis. Leaders must embody the values of openness and collaboration, setting an example for their teams. This includes encouraging employees of all levels to voice their ideas, rewarding risk-taking behavior and creativity, and demonstrating a willingness to engage with external partners. **When employees see their leaders actively embracing collaboration, they are more likely to do so themselves.**

---

[44]Whitehurst, *The Open Organization.*

[45]L. V. Gerstner Jr, *Who Says Elephants Can't Dance?: Leading a Great Enterprise Through Dramatic Change* (Zondervan, 2009).

As Whitehurst notes,[46] he saw his role as one that creates context for people to do their best work, and indeed, leaders must be architects of context, rather than micromanagers. They must create the conditions for openness, where decisions are transparent, information is shared, and people are trusted to act. Here, there must be a change in the perceptions among managers and other stakeholders, and a willingness to examine and reexamine again and again how things are done while being open to change, such as new products, new business models, and the use of new and disruptive technologies. The understanding that there are ideas outside of the company walls that could benefit the organization and that it is alright to make mistakes and learn from them is essential.

It is crucial to nurture an entrepreneurial mindset among employees. This involves training programs, workshops, and hackathons that encourage employees to think creatively, take calculated risks, and approach problems with a start-up-like mentality. These activities are necessary tools for fostering a culture of experimentation and for building capacities that will make collaborations more effective. Encouraging employees to dedicate a portion of their time to exploring innovative new ideas through side projects, much like Google's famed "20% time," can also be highly effective. For Google, examples such as Gmail, AdSense, and numerous other projects are often cited as results of this initiative. **This is an excellent model for idea generation, but when it comes to implementation at scale, organizations should leverage this ability in conjunction with partnerships and collaboration.**

Coca-Cola is another example of a company that has demonstrated a strong commitment to open innovation through various activities, including its successful partnership in Israel, "The Bridge by Coca-Cola," a six-month commercialization program for tech start-ups. It provides guidance and networking opportunities without requiring the acquisition of equity. The program has enabled Coca-Cola to integrate innovative solutions in several fields, including consumer data management and digital transformation, improving efficiency. The program was founded by Alan Boehme, CTO of the company, in partnership with Gabby Czertok,

---

[46]J. Whitehurst, "I Believe My Role Is to Create Context for People to Do Their Best Work," [Interview]. *The Exco Group*, August 19, 2020.

founder of The Builders, and was supported by Ed Steinike (CIO) and Muhtar Kent (chairman and CEO) at The Coca-Cola Company, such level of senior sponsorship in partnership with business and start-up expertise allowed a deep integration and understanding of the business problems as well as the start-up opportunities and with a high level of trust on both sides increased chances of success.

While it is difficult without proper guidance, organizations must adapt to today's business landscape. This can be done through innovation workshops and pilots. **Based on my experience, in the first two years, the only KPI that matters should be the number of pilots conducted, without measuring their ROI.** Measuring innovation by ROI at this early stage is a fundamental and destructive mistake that I have seen many managers make due to a lack of perspective and understanding of open innovation. Without realizing it, they unintentionally kill innovation from the very beginning and shut down valuable and promising initiatives. This approach, which focuses instead on the number of pilots, is supported by multinationals operating in Israel, where 57 percent cite[47] the number of collaborations, PoCs, and facilitated partnerships as their key innovation metric, far surpassing conversion rates, financial returns, patents, sales, and other KPIs. **Real return on investment should only be assessed in the third year, once the innovation culture is fully embedded.**

Human resource departments play a crucial role in recruiting and training employees and managers motivated by a fear of missing out (FOMO) mentality, rather than skeptical, risk-averse, and close-minded employees who are convinced they already know everything. **These employees and managers block decisions and ideas that are "Not Invented Here" (NIH) and are detrimental to the future of any organization, as they unrealistically believe that what worked in the past will continue to work in the future. Let me use this important topic as an alert to all readers—it will not.** Therefore, making the needed changes in your organization and removing such people from decision-making positions is critical.

It is also worth noting that innovation also has an additional inbound benefit in the human resource aspect. My experience shows that

[47]PwC Israel, "The State of Innovation."

employees and managers involved in the innovation process are more loyal and connected to their organization. It is therefore vital to motivate, incentivize, and accept failures in the process.

Common Open Innovation Pitfalls: Speed Versus Structure

Start-ups move fast, while corporations prioritize stability. This mismatch creates frustration for both sides. Imagine a large retail corporation partnering with an AI start-up to enhance customer analytics. The start-up expects to roll out a prototype in six weeks, but the corporation's procurement and IT security reviews took six months.

Solutions:

- Implement a separate, expedited approval framework for pilots and proof of concepts, cutting unnecessary delays in procurement, compliance, and legal reviews.
- Establish a clear service-level agreement (SLA) for approvals (e.g., contracts signed in 30 days, pilot results reviewed in 60 days).
- Assign a dedicated corporate head of innovation who can navigate internal bottlenecks to prevent start-ups from getting lost in bureaucracy.

Human resource departments should also attempt to recruit employees from start-up companies for relevant roles. The more employees in the organization have experience with start-up companies, the more willing they will be to take risks and experiment, and the more innovation will occur both internally and through external sources. HR leaders are increasingly recognizing the need to recruit such talent, and when faced with candidates of similar qualifications, organizations are increasingly favoring those with start-up backgrounds.

To foster the right kind of culture, there should also be clear communication depicting the organization's vision and goals regarding innovation. Employees need to understand not only what the organization is trying to achieve but also how and why collaborations with external entities are critical to its success. This kind of transparency further helps align internal stakeholders with the broader strategy, making them active participants in the company's innovation journey.

Equally important, innovation must be clearly linked to compensation and rewards. Employees should see that creative thinking, successful experimentation, and meaningful contributions to innovation efforts are recognized and financially incentivized. This alignment ensures that risk-taking and collaboration are not only encouraged but are in fact rewarded.

Moreover, by exposing more employees to collaboration with start-ups, organizations foster greater openness, agility, creativity, and a willingness to engage with diverse mindsets that are often absent in traditional corporate environments.

This however, is not enough. Ultimately, **corporations must learn to speak the start-up lingo**. This means that to be an attractive partner, an organization needs to remove bureaucratic barriers and understand that start-ups do not have the time for their partners to move slowly. The quote below, said to me by a start-up that was in touch with a large traditional company, is an example of a mindset that needs to change. Start-ups no longer compete over working with corporations; instead, the latter now compete over start-ups (Figure 11.1).

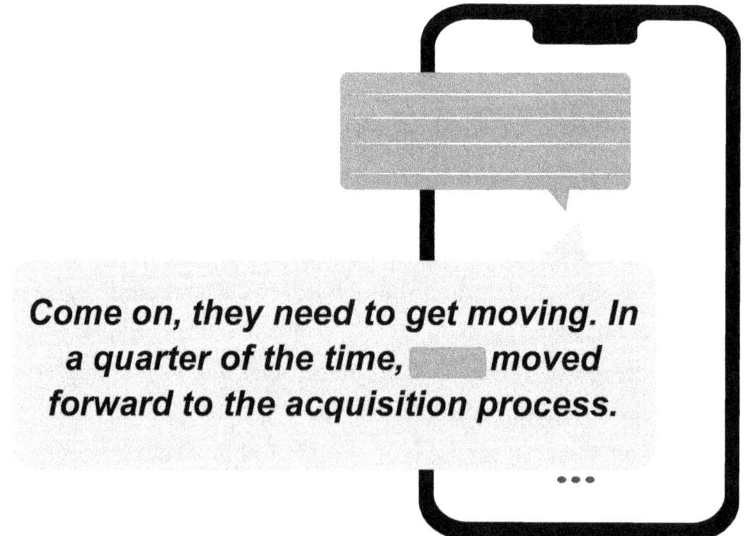

Figure 11.1 The cost of slow decision making

In fact, the need to speak the start-up lingo could not be greater. **Many partnerships fail because of cultural mismatches, including differences in organizational pace, decision-making structures, communication styles, and attitudes toward risk.** These can lead to frustration, inefficiencies, and ultimately, failed innovation efforts.

A good example that illustrates this is the failed AOL–Time Warner merger, a notably disastrous corporate deal.

Common Open Innovation Pitfalls: Formality Versus Agility

Corporations rely on structured reporting, scheduled meetings, and hierarchical decision making, while start-ups operate in real time, favoring informal discussions, quick iterations, and flat decision-making structures. Consider a cybersecurity start-up partnering with a large bank to develop a fraud detection system. The start-up expected biweekly check-ins, while the bank's IT team provided quarterly reports.

Solutions:

- Agree on which updates require formal reports, and which can be handled through real-time collaboration tools (e.g., WhatsApp, Slack, Notion, or Trello).
- Use biweekly touchpoints to align progress and address issues early.
- Have corporate employees spend time at the start-up's office, and vice versa, to build mutual understanding of working styles and improve the level of engagement of all parties.

In January 2000, AOL and Time Warner announced a merger valued at a combined market capitalization of $350 billion, the largest in U.S. history at the time. The deal was intended to revolutionize media by fusing Time Warner's traditional content empire with AOL's Internet-driven distribution model, with both sides calling it a historic moment that will create unprecedented media access and immense economic growth possibilities. AOL—the younger, smaller, and more innovative player—was merged into the traditional Time Warner corporation to bring innovation and new business opportunities. **The two companies shared strategic goals but were culturally incompatible.** Richard Parsons, then-president of Time Warner, later admitted:

> I remember saying at a vital board meeting where we approved this, that life was going to be different going forward because they're very different cultures, but I have to tell you, I underestimated how different ... The business model sort of collapsed under us, and then finally this cultural matter. As I said, it was beyond certainly my abilities to figure out how to blend the old media and the new media culture. They were like different species, and in fact, they were species that were inherently at war.[48]

Common Open Innovation Pitfalls: Aligning Tolerance Levels

Start-ups thrive on experimentation, while corporations prioritize risk mitigation, compliance, and long-term stability. Corporations may thus abandon promising projects too early, while start-ups may push forward without adequate safeguards. Imagine a biotech start-up working on AI-driven drug discovery solution with a global pharmaceutical leader. The start-up aims to launch a real-world pilot using patient data within months, but the corporation's legal team insists on two years of regulatory pretrials.

Solutions:

- Establish an isolated test environment where start-ups can experiment without regulatory or operational risks.
- Define acceptable levels of failure, including which failures are tolerable and which require oversight.
- Implement milestone-based project and funding, where investments increase as key objectives are met.

[48] T. Arango, "In Retrospect: How the AOL-Time Warner Merger Went So Wrong," *The New York Times*, January 10, 2010.

AOL's fast-moving, disruptive mindset clashed with Time Warner's traditional, hierarchical decision-making process, and while AOL pursued aggressive growth strategies, Time Warner was risk-averse and compliance-driven. The two companies also suffered from internal power struggles and mistrust, which led to internal sabotage.

The result? Job losses, financial decimation, SEC and Department of Justice investigations, and one of the worst stock collapses in history, with the combined company's value shrinking by 2008 to one-seventh of its worth at the time of the merger.

This merger was not doomed by market conditions or poor strategies but rather because of a failure to align how the two companies worked together.

This cultural misalignment derails many corporate–start-up partnerships, research collaborations, and innovation ventures on a daily basis. In my years of working with corporations, I encountered many organizations with the right idea—they wanted to collaborate—but made the same mistake, not realizing that they must change their company's DNA to succeed. **Even the most promising partnerships will fail when speed, risk appetite, communication, and leadership styles are ignored.**

Corporations must understand that start-ups are not waiting in line to work with them, which is why they must be transparent, attentive, respectful, and available for the start-up, ready to make quick decisions and ensure that their processes are fast, simple, and effective. Otherwise, they will risk losing the partnership to their competition (Figure 11.2).

This quote was taken from a conversation I had with one of my clients and illustrates a mindset that must change for open innovation to succeed. **Corporations must see start-ups not as suppliers but as partners.** This means, among other things, paying start-ups for their services immediately, not in 60 or 90 days. Doing so demonstrates an understanding of the start-up's cash flow realities, and when itis there, entrepreneurs talk about it in the ecosystem, spreading the word to other start-ups in a ripple effect, allowing the corporation to become more attractive as a potential partner.

Corporations should therefore offer paid pilots, for example, even when start-ups are willing to conduct ones for free. Insisting on payment sends a strong message of respect and partnership, as no one should

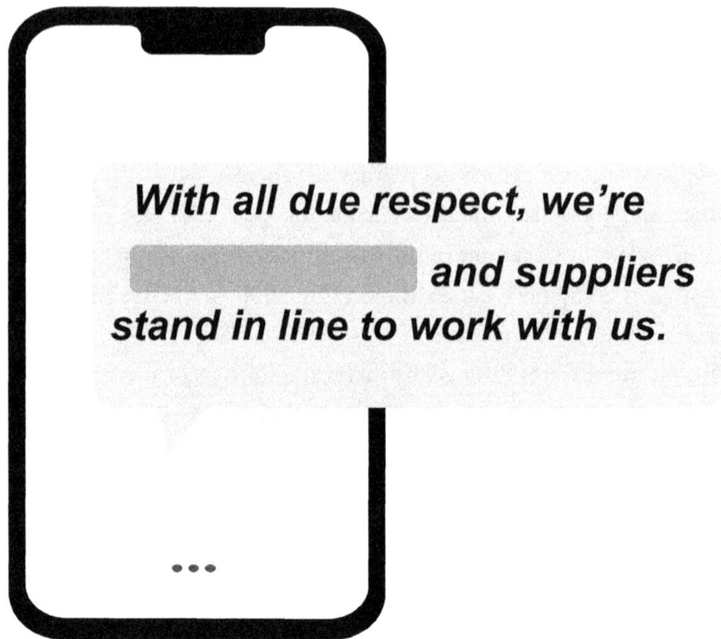

Figure 11.2 A misguided sense of corporate leverage

be expected to work for free. This kind of commitment spreads virally throughout the ecosystem and builds a reputation that attracts top startups, giving the organization a first-mover advantage on the best and newest ideas.

Corporations should also understand that innovation costs money, and that the budget will most likely originate from management during the first two years, and the following years from the P&L of the different business units benefiting from innovation. This does not mean that the company must spend large sums; in open innovation, these are usually smaller sums intended to deliver proof of concept. **Another key advantage is that when funding comes from the business units themselves, it increases their engagement, helps harness mid-level managers, and encourages success.**

Cultural misalignment is one of the most underestimated risks in open innovation, yet it is one of the most critical factors in achieving success. Organizations can bridge cultural gaps and create long-term, high-impact innovation partnerships by proactively assessing cultural fit, establishing structured alignment strategies, and continuously managing the partnership.

Common Open Innovation Pitfalls: Power Struggles and Leadership Conflicts

Many partnerships fail because leaders compete for control instead of collaborating.

Consider AOL and Time Warner. Here, AOL executives believed they were in control due to their higher stock valuation, while Time Warner executives resented being overshadowed despite their legacy dominance. This infighting stalled decision making, leading to paralysis.

Solutions:

- Define who has decision-making power, who manages execution, and how conflicts will be resolved before the partnership begins.
- Establish a neutral partnership board that includes executives from both sides, ensuring balanced decision making.
- Define structured escalation pathways to resolve disputes before they derail the project.

Companies that invest in cultural alignment with their partners will always be better partners for open innovation and will integrate innovation more effectively.

By prioritizing a collaborative culture and investing in cultural alignment, corporations can create an environment where internal teams and external partners feel valued and empowered, setting the stage for successful, transformative partnerships. However, changing the mindset alone is not enough; to become an attractive partner, organizations must also make structural changes.

This will not only result in the organization becoming a more attractive partner for collaboration but will also make the collaborations themselves more effective, as will be discussed in the following chapter.

CHAPTER 12

Streamlining Structures for Effective Partnerships

We try to create teams that are no larger than can be fed with two pizzas.

—Jeff Bezos

For corporations seeking to successfully engage in open innovation and establish effective partnerships, having the proper structure is as crucial **as having the right mindset**. Even the most forward-thinking organizations can struggle to form successful partnerships if their internal processes are slow, bureaucratic, or misaligned with the fast-moving nature of start-ups and other external innovators, who are, more often than not, more agile than corporations. To truly benefit from open innovation, these often larger and more traditional players must streamline their structures, simplify decision making, and remove unnecessary barriers that prevent effective collaboration.

Amazon's approach to this is particularly noteworthy. One of its most famous models is the "two-pizza teams" concept, which Jeff Bezos implemented to ensure agility and efficiency. The idea behind this approach is simple: If a team cannot be fed with two pizzas, it is too large. This structure allows teams to remain small, autonomous, and focused on solving specific problems. This approach fosters a start-up-like mentality within the corporation, with independent teams free to develop new ideas, test them rapidly, and iterate based on feedback.

In fact, studies support this notion, and a recent study[49] which covered 25 international corporations that participated in 10 acceleration

[49]M. Banka, N. Chmiel, M. Kostrzewski, et al., "Understanding Corporate Concerns. Barriers and Challenges in Corporate–Start-Up Collaboration," *Journal of Open Innovation: Technology, Market, and Complexity* 10, no. 4 (2024): 100388.

programs in Poland[50] suggested that mature companies characterized by complex and well-established structures face challenges in promoting external and internal innovation. The study notes that insufficient flexibility, organizational rigidity, and excessive focus on procedural issues are some of the key factors hindering partnerships with start-ups. **The study also suggests that large companies interested in establishing relationships with start-ups must take steps to develop appropriate tools and rules that will allow them to interact with start-ups.** Some of the main barriers identified in the research included, among other things:

- Lack of start-up collaboration strategy and procedures by corporations. Corporations lacking a structured collaboration strategy for start-ups hinder successful partnerships.
- Difficulty identifying suitable corporate innovation ambassadors and champions for start-up engagement, understanding their needs, products, services, and technologies. This includes decision-making mechanisms and procedures. It was suggested that start-ups may struggle to comprehend and navigate corporate decision making due to communication and relationship barriers.
- Corporations' lack of understanding about start-ups' innovations and processes. Here, the impact was found to be related to both cultural differences and organizational rigidity. This can be solved through training, lectures, and workshops, as well as through meetings with entrepreneurs.
- Red tape—Complex and bureaucratic corporate procedures that slow down start-up collaborations. Proactively involving different teams early on ensures smoother collaboration, faster decision making, and fewer roadblocks.

As a result, the researchers[51] suggested that corporates should focus not only on the differences in culture but also on decision-making

[50]Including PARP, 2019, FundingBox Accelerator, 2018, Blue Dot Solutions, 2019, DGA, 2019, AccelPoint, 2019, Fundacja Polska Przedsiębiorcza, 2021, HugeTECH, 2021, Krakowski Park Technologiczny, 2021, ŁSSE, 2021, Brinc Limited, 2021.

[51]Banka et al., "Understanding Corporate Concerns," 100388.

processes, speed, and expectations of the different parties. This will enable corporations to overcome barriers and achieve successful collaboration, thereby enjoying the advantages that start-ups can offer.

Bureaucratic processes within corporations, particularly in regulated sectors, hinder the initiation and development of partnerships due to the complexity of corporate structures, which act as roadblocks and barriers.[52] Start-ups, in contrast, thrive thanks to their speed and agility, and often make major strategic decisions in mere days, whereas a corporation might take months to make a similar action.

From my experience working with corporations and start-ups alike, **this mismatch frequently leads to failed collaborations, as start-ups and other partners become frustrated with delays, unclear objectives, or excessive bureaucracy**. In fact, a study by McKinsey[53] found that only 28 percent of the start-ups surveyed were completely satisfied with their corporate partner. The main issues found were a lack of speed, too much bureaucracy, and a lack of support on the corporate side, while other studies also include coordination, cultural differences, and contractual issues.[54]

The level of internal buy-in is the defining factor between an organization that successfully drives innovation and one that falls short of its potential. When key stakeholders across departments are aligned and committed to innovation, the organization achieves a significantly higher success rate in transitioning pilots into full-scale implementation. Internal engagement is more than a supporting factor here and is required to move from experimentation to execution and the creation of a tangible business value.

According to BCG research, this misalignment is the reason why 45 percent of corporations are dissatisfied with their partnership with

---

[52]Bureaucratic procedures, particularly in regulated sectors, also hinder the initiation and development of partnerships, with complex corporate structures and regulatory environments acting as roadblocks.

[53]K. Dörner, M. Flötotto, T. Henz, and T. Stralin, "You Can't Buy Love Reimagining Corporate-Startup Partnerships in the DACH Region," *McKinsey & Company*, October 2020.

[54]S. Bannerjee, S. Bielli, and C. Haley, *Scaling Together: Overcoming Barriers in Corporate-Startup Collaboration* (Nesta, 2016).

start-ups.[55] Worse still, corporate executives, seeing little ROI from such failed innovative initiatives, may become skeptical about working with start-ups altogether.

Furthermore, **internal misalignment within corporations can be just as damaging as external inefficiencies**. When different departments operate in silos, partnerships become fragmented, lacking clear ownership and accountability. A start-up might engage with a corporation's innovation team, only to discover that the legal, finance, product, or IT departments have entirely different requirements, creating bottlenecks that derail the initiative. This often results in start-ups getting discouraged and abandoning the collaboration before it yields results.

Luckily, I have found that these issues can be solved through actions that may sound complicated but, in truth, can be easily achieved with proper guidance. To successfully partner for innovation, the corporate side of the equation must first understand that start-ups cannot wait for their more bureaucratic partners and that the latter must design their internal structures to be agile, transparent, and partnership-friendly.

Lessons Learned from Corporate Giants and Their Start-Up Collaborations: Google and Motorola

In 2012, Google acquired Motorola Mobility for $12.5 billion, with the intention of integrating its hardware expertise into the Android ecosystem. However, two years later, Google sold Motorola to Lenovo for $2.9 billion, marking this a major and high-profile acquisition failure.

As a software-driven company, Google faced challenges in managing Motorola's hardware-focused operations, which had a more bureaucratic culture than Google's innovative and flexible one.

What Went Wrong?

1. Cultural mismatch, as Google struggled to manage Motorola's hardware-focused operations

[55]M. Brigl, S. Cross-Selbeck, N. Dehnert, F. Schmieg, & S. Simon, "After the Honeymoon Ends: Making Corporate-Startup Relationships Work," *Boston Consulting Group*, June 13, 2019.

2. There was a lack of a clear strategy on whether Google acquired Motorola for its patents, devices, or both.
3. This was a case of poor postacquisition execution, with Motorola not being given the level of independence needed to succeed.

Some key tactics that can assist corporations in this endeavor include:

- Centralized Innovation Hubs—Many successful corporations establish a dedicated open innovation unit as a single point of contact for external innovators. This team bridges the gap between start-ups, academia, and corporations, ensuring smooth communication and alignment. In fact, according to recent data, 89 percent of European corporates that managed collaborations using a dedicated business unit achieved their objectives.[56]
- Defined Roles and Responsibilities—clearly outlining the roles of each partner within the governance structure. This clarity helps prevent misunderstandings and ensures accountability throughout the partnerships.
- Breaking Down Silos—encouraging cross-departmental initiatives that promote relationship-building among employees from different teams. For example, regular meetings where leaders from various departments discuss their objectives and challenges allow them to identify areas where departments can support one another. Another less formal activity can be a virtual coffee chat, which can help build trust and foster informal connections.
- Fast-Track Approval Processes—streamline decision-making frameworks to allow promising partnerships to move forward quickly. For example, setting up a "fast-track" approval mechanism for start-up collaborations with the needed corporate leaders on board and available.
- Cross-Functional Teams—Instead of leaving partnerships solely in the hands of innovation teams, companies should involve key stakeholders from across the corporation early. These include key

[56]Sopra Steria Scale, "Open Innovation Report 2023."

personnel from legal, compliance, and different business units, depending on the specific sector, ensuring that potential roadblocks are addressed proactively rather than as potential last-minute dealbreakers.

- Soliciting Feedback on Communication Processes—Companies should create channels for employees to provide feedback. This input can improve how teams interact on new initiatives, ultimately enhancing collaboration across the organization.
- Flexible Procurement and Contracting—Many corporations have rigid procurement policies that are ill-suited for working with start-ups. Companies should adopt simplified agreements tailored for early-stage companies instead of lengthy, complex contracts designed for large vendors. One key suggestion is introducing "pilot contracts" that allow for low-risk, short-term engagements with start-ups before committing to full-scale adoption. In my experience, this is key for successful innovation. Moreover, following a successful pilot and implementation within the organization, it is crucial to explore the start-up's relevance to other departments and challenges across the corporation. A single start-up can often provide solutions to multiple areas of the business, and maximizing its value requires internal awareness and coordination.
- KPIs That Reflect Innovation Goals—Traditional performance metrics often fail to capture the value of external partnerships. Instead of measuring success solely by revenue or cost savings, corporations should track metrics like speed to market, pilot conversion rates, number of pilots, and ecosystem engagement to ensure they foster a productive innovation culture.

These many adaptations needed by the corporation may seem overwhelming. A good first step would be to conduct a "structural audit" of the company to examine possible changes required, including introducing an internal innovation champion. And above all, based on my experience, **a corporation that wishes to collaborate with start-ups must learn to think and speak like a start-up. A start-up will never adopt corporate lingo, and once this is understood, everything becomes easier.**

In recent years, the need to formalize innovation practices has also been recognized at the global standards level. The newly introduced ISO 56001 standard, focused on Innovation Management Systems, provides organizations with a practical framework for embedding innovation into their culture and operations. Rather than treating innovation as a series of isolated projects, ISO 56001 offers a structured, auditable approach for integrating innovation strategy, processes, and metrics across the enterprise. For companies pursuing open innovation, this standard can serve as a powerful guide for aligning leadership, governance, and cross-departmental collaboration with internationally accepted best practices, ensuring that innovation is not only encouraged but consistently executed and measured, while assisting with their internal structural audits.

Companies that have successfully streamlined their structures for open innovation offer valuable lessons. For example, BMW's Startup Garage operates under a "venture client" model, enabling start-ups to test their technologies within BMW's ecosystem without complexity. This means that instead of requiring a full-scale procurement process, BMW provides start-ups with a rapid, low-friction pathway to test and validate their technologies within its ecosystem, purchasing a first unit of the start-up's technology, product, or service, and pilot it with no equity. This means the start-up receives a supplier status, with no investment in the processes of the company itself. This dramatically reduces friction for the corporation and the start-ups and allows BMW to integrate technological solutions more efficiently. Similarly, Unilever Foundry offers start-ups an opportunity to work with the company through a structured but flexible framework, reducing corporate red tape while ensuring strategic alignment with the company's priorities.

At the heart of effective open innovation lies the ability to move fast and remove friction. A corporation that is easy to work with will attract the best start-ups, researchers, and external innovators who wish to work with it. In contrast, those with inefficient processes will find that the most promising opportunities pass them by in favor of more agile competitors and tomorrow's market leaders.

By simplifying structures, fostering internal alignment, and enabling rapid decision making, corporations can become true innovation partners, leveraging external talent, technologies, and ideas to drive a long-term competitive advantage.

To remain competitive, companies must take immediate action.

The companies that thrive in the coming years will be those that don't just talk about innovation but actively remove barriers that prevent it from happening. The time to act is now.

CHAPTER 13

Establishing Trust and Reducing Barriers

I see Silicon Valley as a "community of trust." It has people with ideas, funds and technologies. It is an ecosystem built on mutual trust.

—Yoshikuni Takashige

It takes more than technological capabilities or financial resources to conduct open innovation successfully. Collaboration demands fostering trust, transparency, and agility in interactions with start-ups, research institutions, and other key external stakeholders in the ecosystem. Trust is the foundation of every successful partnership, and corporations that fail to cultivate it will struggle to attract and retain valuable collaborators. In fact, research on open innovation partnerships demonstrates that mutual trust is a successful predictor of successful open innovation.[57]

It is vital to communicate clearly and consistently with innovation partners to build trust. Start-ups often hesitate to engage with large organizations due to concerns about slow decision-making processes, bureaucratic hurdles, and a lack of transparency regarding expectations and internal procedures. **Corporations must actively address these concerns by establishing clear engagement processes, setting realistic expectations, and providing dedicated points of contact, such as a head of innovation.**

Establishing a formal innovation engagement framework, such as a dedicated innovation office, start-up liaison teams, or structured onboarding programs, can help remove uncertainty and create a more inviting

[57]M. Fang, L. Cai, K. Park, and M. Su, "Trust (in) Congruence, Open Innovation, and Circular Economy Performance: Polynomial Regression and Response Surface Analyses," *Journal of Environmental Management* 358 (2024): 120930.

environment for external innovators. For example, Philips transformed its approach through its High-Tech Campus in Eindhoven, launched in 2005 as an open innovation hub. Rather than keeping research behind closed doors as it had done at its historic NatLab, Philips deliberately opened its research facilities and partnered with leading R&D organizations. This structural shift required a significant mindset change within Philips' own organization. As Franklin Schuling, Philips' Connected Care Program Manager, stated: "Truth be said, it took some time for our own organization to embrace the concept of open innovation. We were hesitant to share our ideas and know-how." However, by creating a formal, shared research environment with clear engagement models, Philips moved from conducting isolated research to becoming what they term an "innovation orchestration lab" where they bring together external innovation and internal capabilities to create products.[58]

The advantage of this framework is, among other things, responsiveness. As stated, start-ups operate in fast-paced environments where delays in decision making can result in lost opportunities and even lead to a start-up's demise. **Corporations must implement mechanisms to accelerate decision making related to innovation partnerships.** This may include setting predefined response timelines, empowering middle managers to approve pilot projects, and streamlining procurement processes to prevent unnecessary delays.

Trust mechanisms extend beyond organizational structures to include reputation systems and transparent performance indicators. eBay revolutionized online commerce by addressing the fundamental problem of trust between strangers through its reputation system. When eBay launched in 1995, the company recognized that users would not transact with people they didn't know without some mechanism to assess reliability. eBay's solution—which collects, aggregates, and displays feedback about participants' past behavior—proved transformative. While corporate open innovation doesn't require identical reputation mechanics, the principle applies: Corporations should establish visible, verifiable indicators of partnership success. This might include publishing case studies

[58]F. Schuling, "Partnering with Philips to Innovate for a Healthier World: Holst Centre—15 Years of Open Innovation," *Philips*, January 4, 2022.

of successful pilot programs, maintaining publicly accessible innovation partnership dashboards showing response times and project outcomes, or creating recognition programs that highlight successful collaborations. Transparency about past performance, including both successes and lessons learned builds institutional trust.

Transparency in collaboration agreements is equally essential. Many start-ups are hesitant to work with corporations due to concerns over intellectual property rights, revenue-sharing models, and potential conflicts of interest. Organizations should address these concerns head-on by establishing fair and transparent policies that protect the interests of both parties. **Remember—open innovation is about creating mutual benefits, and these start-ups are not just suppliers but key partners.** Clearly defining ownership of codeveloped solutions, ensuring fair value distribution, and committing to ethical collaboration practices will go a long way in building lasting relationships while establishing a strong reputation for your organization within the ecosystem.

Microsoft has established a comprehensive model through its Shared Innovation Initiative,[59] built on explicit principles designed to address precisely these concerns. The initiative rests on clear commitments including: (1) respect for ownership of existing technology, (2) assuring customer ownership of new patents and design rights, (3) support for open source, (4) licensing new IP rights back to Microsoft where appropriate, (5) software portability, (6) transparency and clarity through well-organized and defined processes ensuring customers always have clear and complete information, and (7) learning and improvement. Microsoft explicitly appoints executive sponsors to address questions or issues quickly. This framework directly addresses start-up concerns by making IP ownership unambiguous before collaboration begins.

Excessive internal bureaucracy is a significant barrier to collaboration. Simplifying contract negotiations, offering standardized agreements for pilot programs, and minimizing the number of approvals required can significantly help reduce barriers and foster trust. Cisco's Startup Engagement Platform is an excellent example of a platform that enables start-ups

[59] B. Smith, "A New IP Strategy for a New Era of Shared Innovation," *Official Microsoft Blog*, April 4, 2018.

to collaborate with mentors, investors, and ecosystem partners through a single dashboard, thereby eliminating the friction of coordinating across multiple corporate systems and contacts.

Corporate culture plays a pivotal role in reducing these barriers to collaboration; therefore, fostering a culture that values openness and external engagement is essential, as previously mentioned. Employees, particularly those in leadership and operational roles, **should be encouraged to view innovation partnerships as opportunities rather than risks.** Training programs that educate employees on the benefits of open innovation can help shift mindsets and reduce internal resistance to external partnerships.

Ultimately, corporations that wish to thrive should recognize that trust is not built overnight. Instead, it is cultivated through consistent, reliable actions. The mechanisms that build this trust are concrete and measurable: transparent engagement frameworks with clear response timelines, simplified agreements that protect the interests of both parties, reputation systems that reward partnership quality, and dedicated infrastructure. By reducing barriers, demonstrating a commitment to fair and ethical collaboration, and fostering a culture that truly values external innovation, companies can position themselves as preferred partners for key players in the global innovation ecosystem, leading to growth and a sustained competitive advantage in an era of rapid technological disruption.

CHAPTER 14

Corporate Venture Capital and Other Strategic Tools

"I have not failed. I've just found 10,000 ways that won't work."

—Thomas Edison

The following chapters will act as a practical roadmap for organizations looking to implement open innovation successfully. While previous chapters explored the mindset and structural adjustments required, the next few chapters will focus on proven models and tools that corporations can use to harness external innovation effectively.

Among the most prominent tools, and one that the world's leading corporations have successfully integrated into their innovation strategy, are corporate venture capital arms, incubators, and accelerators. These provide corporations with structured avenues to engage with start-ups through direct investments, mentorship, and, most importantly, pilot programs.

Success Stories in Open Innovation: Airbus

Challenge: Airbus pursued innovation in aerospace technology while reducing development time and costs.

Open Innovation Approach: Airbus BizLab is a global accelerator program that collaborates with start-ups and small- and medium-sized enterprises (SMEs) to develop innovative solutions for aerospace challenges.

Outcome: The program has led to breakthroughs in areas like drone technology and sustainable aviation, enhancing Airbus's innovation pipeline.

Corporate Venture Capital—Unlike traditional venture capital funds, which focus purely on financial returns, corporate venture capital funds are investment vehicles created by corporations to support start-ups that align with their strategic interests. Corporate venture capital serves a dual purpose: achieving strategic objectives while generating financial value. They enable corporations to gain early access to disruptive technologies, explore new business models, and test innovative solutions before full-scale deployment. For example, GV (formerly known as Google Ventures) and Intel Capital are well-known corporate venture capital arms that have helped their parent companies stay ahead of the curve in fields like AI, hardware, and cloud computing.

Accelerators and Incubators, on the other hand, act as controlled environments where start-ups receive resources, industry expertise, and business guidance in exchange for their innovative potential.

Accelerators are typically short-term (usually lasting three to six months), cohort-based programs designed to rapidly scale start-ups that already have a minimum viable product or some market traction. Start-ups receive mentorship, funding, networking, and the chance to present their work to potential investors at a "demo day."

Incubators are longer-term programs that support very early-stage start-ups or even just ideas. These offer shared workspaces, advisory services, and technical resources in a more flexible, non-cohort-based format.

How to Establish an Effective Corporate Venture Capital Program

1. Clearly articulate whether the fund aims to drive new revenue streams, explore emerging technologies, enhance existing products, or any other aim that fits your organization. It could, and often should, fit more than one challenge.
2. Appoint experienced investors who understand both the start-up ecosystem and the corporate world. These investors should clearly understand your needs, challenges, and strategy.
3. Identify industries, technologies, and funding stages that align with corporate priorities.

4. Slow corporate approval processes are harmful for relationships with start-ups. To become attractive partners, corporations must streamline internal procedures and reduce bureaucratic friction.
5. Investing in start-ups is only valuable if the corporation actively collaborates with them through such actions as pilots. Start-ups are your partners and serve as a valuable resource that you should utilize to gain value.

In short: Accelerators help start-ups grow fast. Incubators help them get started.

The success of models like Y Combinator, Techstars, and Plug and Play demonstrates that corporations that invest in start-up ecosystems gain access to new ideas and talent pipelines, often leading to acquisitions or long-term collaborations. Y Combinator, for example, helped launch Airbnb, Dropbox, and Stripe. Plug and Play partners directly with global corporations to run industry-specific accelerators.

Many corporate innovation programs fail to deliver meaningful results due to some common pitfalls that can be avoided with the right approach. One of the biggest challenges is the lack of strategic alignment. Another is slow decision making, while cultural differences also create friction. **Experience shows that when bureaucratic actors participate in such innovation workshops, especially those that result in a pilot with a relevant start-up, they begin to understand the urgency and constraints under which start-ups operate.** Only then do they realize that flexibility and a new approach to risk management are critical.

How to Establish an Effective Accelerator or Incubator

1. Accelerators work best for scaling start-ups, while incubators are ideal for nurturing early-stage ideas. You should understand what your needs are and how these can better help you achieve them.

2. Engaging business units early will ensure alignment and resources for pilots or potential integrations.
3. You should provide start-ups with funding, office space, mentorship, support with scaling up their operations through your network, and perhaps most importantly, direct access to corporate decision makers. Remember—their success is your success.
4. Start-ups move fast, and corporations must match their agility by reducing contractual and procurement red tape.
5. Define KPIs clearly, using such metrics as pilot success rates, product adoption, or start-up acquisitions. These will help measure the success of such programs.

Additionally, providing real business opportunities is key, as if an accelerator or incubator fails to offer market access or meaningful support from the corporate side, start-ups will seek better partnerships elsewhere. Finally, many programs also fall into the trap of measuring the wrong metrics.

While corporate venture capital arms, accelerators, and incubators play a crucial role in corporate innovation, they are only one part of the equation. To maximize their impact, corporations must leverage technological partnerships and collaborative platforms that enable seamless interactions among diverse stakeholders.

CHAPTER 15

Technological Partnerships and Collaborative Platforms

Technology is best when it brings people together.

—Matt Mullenweg

Investing in start-ups, launching accelerators, and initiating actions are powerful open innovation tactics. Yet these efforts are often suboptimal without effective collaboration platforms and technological solutions to support them. Organizations need to do more than find external innovators to partner with; **they should utilize technology to ensure that the knowledge and solutions these partners bring can be efficiently integrated into corporate workflows, thereby supporting innovation processes.**

Technological platforms play a crucial role in streamlining these processes. They enable corporations to identify the right partners, communicate effectively, manage projects in real time, and ensure that innovation is effective and unhindered by bureaucracy. For example, companies that successfully leverage AI-powered scouting platforms, digital communication tools, and cocreation spaces gain a competitive edge by accelerating decision making and integrating external collaboration into their daily operations.

Corporations that wish to be attractive partners cannot rely solely on slow e-mail communications, endless meetings, or cumbersome approval processes. To avoid this, corporations must adopt agile, easy-to-use digital platforms that facilitate direct and transparent communication, matching the speed at which start-ups operate.

Platforms such as Slack, Microsoft Teams, Zoom, and even messaging apps like WhatsApp, Telegram, and Viber are no longer just for internal communication. Instead, they are critical for bridging the gap between corporations and start-ups. Although it may sound somewhat trivial, many organizations overlook their potential, assuming innovation discussions should only occur through formal e-mails or structured corporate tools. However, the reality is that tools like WhatsApp, Telegram, and Viber create informal, fast-moving channels for direct conversations, quick decision making, and instant updates, especially in the early stages of collaboration.

Success Stories in Open Innovation: BMW

Challenge: BMW aimed to enhance automotive innovation in products, services, systems, and processes—for example, in sustainability, by engaging external start-ups.

Open Innovation Approach: BMW Startup Garage provides start-ups access to BMW's expertise and resources for mobility solutions.

Outcome: The program has driven innovations in autonomous driving and smart mobility.

For example, many of my clients prefer to hold their first meetings with start-ups via Zoom rather than in-person, to streamline communication and move forward quickly. **Companies that utilize messaging tools alongside formal collaboration tools, such as Microsoft Teams, Slack, and Notion, ensure that conversations remain dynamic and actionable.** Setting up dedicated groups or channels in WhatsApp, Telegram, or Viber for each innovation initiative, where corporate leaders, start-up founders, and key project stakeholders can quickly share updates, significantly reduces communication bottlenecks and accelerates progress, while also contributing to increased engagement and involvement.

Beyond messaging tools, **organizations, especially those with 10,000 employees or more, should integrate project management platforms with real-time visibility into innovation initiatives.** Platforms like Trello, Asana, and Monday.com allow corporate innovation teams to track project milestones, assign tasks, and ensure accountability. One best practice is creating a shared dashboard where corporate teams and external innovators can view the status of joint projects, track progress, and raise concerns proactively. This minimizes the risk of start-ups feeling lost in corporate bureaucracy and allows organizations to respond quickly to challenges before they escalate.

Another component of a successful collaboration strategy is leveraging AI-powered scouting and matchmaking platforms. Instead of relying solely on traditional networking events or personal connections, **corporations can utilize technology-driven platforms to identify the most relevant start-ups, research institutions, and emerging technologies in real time.** Some of the most effective platforms include Wellspring and ITONICS. Corporations can utilize these platforms to identify more effective start-up partners and gain strategic insights into the technological trends that are shaping their industry.

However, while these platforms offer powerful search capabilities and real-time data, they can only complement, rather than replace, a dedicated innovation adviser who is an inseparable part of the ecosystem, has a deep understanding of it, and has fast access to key players.

Successful innovators can also invest in digital innovation hubs, where internal teams, start-ups, and external experts can cocreate solutions. Corporations can create digital environments where global teams can brainstorm, prototype, and refine ideas in real time using platforms like Miro and MURAL. A practical approach is to host regular virtual "Innovation Sprints," where start-ups and corporate teams collaborate on short, focused problem-solving sessions. These sprints help corporations avoid endless meetings and long decision cycles by prioritizing execution over discussion.

How to Ensure That Technological Platforms Are Fully Embraced?

To ensure that technological partnerships and collaborative platforms are utilized effectively, corporations should:

1. Train employees and executives on collaboration tools through hands-on workshops and onboarding sessions.
2. Incentivize engagement, rewarding both employees and business units for successfully integrating start-up technologies or collaborating effectively with external partners.

3. Make platforms part of the corporate workflow, with clear expectations set by leadership.
4. Track engagement and optimize usage through regularly measuring adoption rates, participation in innovation projects, and sharing success stories. This can often be done by heads of innovation creating chat groups on platforms such as WhatsApp, where they regularly share updates on innovation they have seen or implemented with colleagues committed to innovation.

Technology partnerships are not limited to corporate–start-up interactions—as we have discussed before, many of the most groundbreaking innovations come from cross-industry collaborations and open data-sharing initiatives. For example, automotive companies are increasingly partnering with AI firms, telecommunications providers, and smart city initiatives to create connected transportation ecosystems. Similarly, companies in the health care and financial services sectors are leveraging blockchain-based platforms and AI-driven analytics tools to enhance security, improve customer experience, and detect fraud more effectively. **To maximize these opportunities, organizations should actively participate in industry consortia, cross-sector working groups, and joint R&D initiatives, and adopt technological solutions that facilitate safer and more efficient data sharing**, such as data anonymization solutions, APIs, and similar tools.

Companies must utilize the right collaboration tools for their specific needs and ensure proper usage to reap their benefits, but that is often not enough. Even with the best technological platforms in place, internal adoption remains one of the biggest barriers to success. Many corporate teams resist using new tools due to a lack of training, uncertainty about their value, or simply due to inertia.

Technology partnerships and collaborative platforms are enablers of open innovation, serving an important role in making it scalable, repeatable, and results-driven. Corporations can increase the likelihood of their efforts succeeding through such tools. Corporations that successfully integrate such tools gain a boost to their innovation efforts, earning a further competitive advantage through promising start-up partnerships.

CHAPTER 16

Strategies for Managing Risk in Collaborative Ventures

The biggest risk is not taking any risk ... In a world that's changing really quickly, the only strategy that is guaranteed to fail is not taking risks.

—Mark Zuckerberg

Innovation, by its nature, involves uncertainty, and when companies engage in collaborative ventures, the risks only multiply. **While external partnerships offer access to fresh ideas, new technologies, and expanded market opportunities, they also introduce challenges such as misalignment between partners, intellectual property concerns, regulatory hurdles, and cultural friction.** If left unmanaged, these risks can derail promising initiatives.

Risk-averse corporate cultures may struggle to trust external partners, while bureaucratic hurdles can slow decision making in joint ventures. To successfully innovate, companies must embrace a structured, dedicated risk management approach that allows for agility without exposing themselves to unnecessary vulnerabilities.

Here are some of the key risks in collaborative innovation:

1. Strategic Misalignment—A partnership can falter if both parties have different goals, risk appetites, or success timelines. A large corporation may prioritize long-term scalability, while a start-up focuses on rapid iteration and market entry.
    - Example: A multinational insurance firm partners with a fintech start-up to streamline claims processing. The start-up

values speed and experimentation, while compliance regulations constrain the insurer. Without alignment, the project stalls.
  - Mitigation: Conduct joint strategy workshops before formalizing partnerships to ensure both parties align objectives, expectations, and KPIs.

2. Intellectual Property and Ownership Disputes—Conflicts may hinder progress without clear agreements on ownership of codeveloped solutions.
   - Example: A health care insurer codevelops an AI-powered fraud detection system with a software vendor. Both later claim ownership, leading to legal disputes.
   - Mitigation: Draft clear IP agreements before initiating collaboration, defining ownership rights, licensing models, and revenue-sharing structures.
3. Regulatory and Compliance Risks—Particularly in highly regulated industries such finance and health, navigating compliance across jurisdictions is a significant hurdle.
   - Example: A European bank partnering with a U.S.-based fintech faces compliance challenges due to differing data privacy laws (GDPR versus U.S. state laws).
   - Mitigation: Establish a regulatory task force within the partnership to proactively monitor and address compliance risks.
4. Operational and Cultural Differences—Large enterprises and start-ups operate at vastly different speeds and have contrasting risk-taking cultures. Without adaptation, friction arises.
   - Example: A corporate R&D team follows rigid approval processes, while their start-up partner iterates rapidly. The mismatch leads to delays.
   - Mitigation: Implement a "bridge team" composed of members from both organizations to ensure smooth collaboration and resolve process misalignments quickly.

Companies should integrate structured risk management into their innovation frameworks to successfully navigate these risks while maintaining agility. Here are some practical tips for mitigating risk in collaborative innovation:

1. Establish a Risk-Impact Framework:
   - Use a Risk-Impact Matrix to categorize potential risks based on likelihood and severity.
   - Regularly update risk registers to monitor evolving threats.
   - Appoint a Risk Champion within the innovation team to oversee partnership risk management.
2. Build Agile Yet Secure Partnership Agreements:
   - Utilize modular contracts allowing for phased collaboration, providing exit options if goals are unmet.
   - Implement performance-based milestones, ensuring funding and resources are released incrementally based on results.
   - Define clear escalation paths for resolving conflicts early.
3. Adopt a Pilot-First Approach:
   - Start with low-risk pilot projects before committing to full-scale integration.
   - Use "sandbox" environments for testing before exposing core business operations to the partnership.
   - Conduct periodic joint retrospectives to assess learnings and refine collaboration processes.
4. Leverage Governance Through Dedicated Innovation Councils:
   - Form an innovation committee composed of stakeholders from both organizations to oversee the partnership's progress.
   - Assign cross-functional teams to continuously evaluate technological, financial, and regulatory risks.

Rather than viewing risk as a deterrent, companies should treat it as a lever for strategic growth. Businesses that successfully integrate structured risk management into their innovation strategies make better decisions, allocating resources more effectively and achieving measurable collaboration success.

Managing risk effectively not only prevents failures but also sets the stage for measuring the impact of innovation. Companies that proactively track risk reduction in their partnerships can quantify success by evaluating such factors as:

- The number of pilots and the number of successful pilots
- Reduction in project failure rates
- Speed of product development cycles
- Financial returns on innovation investments
- Compliance adherence in highly regulated environments

As this book progresses, we will revisit the topic of measuring success, exploring how organizations can develop clear frameworks to assess the outcomes of their open innovation strategies and ensure they drive real business value.

CHAPTER 17

Engaging Leadership in Open Innovation

Innovation distinguishes between a leader and a follower.

—Steve Jobs

Open innovation requires leadership to be actively engaged and an integral part of the process. Too often, innovation initiatives are treated as side projects, lacking the executive sponsorship and strategic integration needed to make a real impact. Without leadership buy-in, even the most promising opportunities will struggle to gain traction, as lower-ranking employees would not be fully invested.

Engaging leadership in open innovation requires a deliberate approach. **It starts with ensuring that the C-suite and board of directors not only endorse innovation but actively champion it.** The leadership's role is not just to approve budgets or attend occasional innovation summits but to create the conditions for innovation to thrive. While grassroots innovation efforts can generate some valuable ideas, **true transformation requires active engagement from the C-suite and board of directors, whose role and mandate are to steer the company through complex waters.** This includes aligning innovation efforts with corporate strategy, fostering a culture of risk-taking, and ensuring cross-functional collaboration.

Leadership involvement ensures that innovation is not just an experiment happening on the sidelines but a core strategic priority fully integrated into the company's vision, operations, and decision-making processes, enabling effective strategy execution.

I always present this crystal-clear paradox to corporate leaders: Investing in innovation comes with the risk of failure, but failing to innovate is an even greater risk and could, and most likely would, lead to market irrelevance.

Despite the urgency, many corporate leaders lack the necessary tools and expertise to effectively navigate the complexities of open innovation. Studies repeatedly show that board members and C-suite executives often undervalue or misunderstand the importance of innovation, failing to take the necessary steps to drive innovation. At the same time, other studies reveal that innovation consistently ranks among the top three corporate priorities[60] and is widely seen as one of the most effective ways to gain a competitive advantage. Decision makers must internalize this reality to be fully harnessed and to champion innovation across their organizations effectively.

For example, a Harvard Business School study found that only 30 percent of board members ranked innovation as a top concern, and merely 21 percent considered technological trends a priority.[61] Similarly, a McKinsey report showed that only 16 percent of directors understood the changing dynamics of their industries, and only 17 percent actively promoted new initiatives.[62] This can easily be explained by the fact that the average age of S&P 1500 directors is 63,[63] with "next-gen" directors, meaning, younger directors who are more likely to have a technology background, standing at 14 percent of the class of 2024, and the average age of new directors in the current class has slightly risen from 58 to 58.2 during the last year.[64]

At the same time, while 83 percent of companies rank innovation among their top three priorities,[65] only 32 percent of directors feel as if their boards have the right mix of skills and expertise to guide corporations forward. 43 percent of executives, for example, noted that boards

---

[60]Boston Consulting Group, "83% of Companies Rank Innovation."

[61]M. Blanding, "Everyone Knows Innovation Is Essential to Business Success—Except Board Directors," *Harvard Business School Working Knowledge*, January 3, 2019.

[62]H. Sarrazin and P. Willmott, "Adapting Your Board to the Digital Age," *McKinsey & Company*, July 13, 2016.

[63]A. Giblin, "IN-DEPTH: Age Diversity in Sharper Focus as Boards Examine Composition," *Diligent*, February 7, 2025.

[64]Spencer Stuart, "2024 S&P 500 New Director and Diversity Snapshot," 2024, https://www.spencerstuart.com/-/media/2024/08/ssbi-director-diversity-snapshot/2024-sp-500-new-director-and-diversity-snapshot.pdf.

[65]Boston Consulting Group, "83% of Companies Rank Innovation."

should include more people with AI and GenAI skills, while only 10 percent of directors mentioned that their boards will add people with such skills in the next 12 months. When asked about how boards should evolve over the next five years, the top three needs, reported by C-level executives, are: investing in board education and development (37 percent), encouraging innovation and forward thinking (36 percent), and enhancing digital literacy and understanding of emerging technologies (34 percent).[66] These data are unsurprising, as previous data showed that while three out of four directors previously claimed that while their corporation has a vision for innovation, innovation is not on the board members' daily agenda, and 57 percent of the directors previously reported that they do not even know how much the corporation invests in research and development, while almost all directors stating that they lack relevant scientific and technological expertise.[67] **The consequences of this leadership gap could not be more severe for any organization; companies that fail to resolve these issues will soon become irrelevant.**

Unsurprisingly, an MIT study of 1,200 publicly traded companies found that organizations with at least three board members with digital and technological expertise outperformed their peers significantly, with 17 percent higher profit margins, 38 percent greater revenue growth, and 34 percent higher market value growth.[68] This demonstrates that **companies led by digitally savvy boards are better equipped to integrate innovation into corporate strategy and translate it into tangible business success.** Since it is the mandate of the board to create a vision and roadmap for organizations and ensure that they generate as much profit as possible for their stakeholders, they must have the tools and skills that enable them to do so.

Clearly, in most cases, boards are not yet fully equipped to innovate. In Israel, regulators have recognized this issue and the importance of technological leadership. In 2018, the Israeli Banking Supervisor,

---

[66] PwC & The Conference Board, "Board Effectiveness: A Survey of the C-Suite," 2025.

[67] Australian Institute of Company Directors, "Driving Innovation: The Boardroom Gap," September 2019.

[68] P. Weill, T. Apel, S. L. Woerner, and J. S. Banner, "It Pays to Have a Digitally Savvy Board," *MIT Sloan Management Review* 60, no. 3 (2019): 41–45.

Dr. Hedva Ber, mandated that banks appoint directors with expertise in technology and innovation. **This unprecedented move was designed to ensure that leadership understands the implications of technological change.** This regulation, which was direly needed, underscores an important fact: boards must evolve to remain relevant. Otherwise, they will fail to effectively govern and ultimately jeopardize the long-term success of the organizations they oversee.

To be effective in this new role, the modern board should therefore:

1. Advance the directors' technological and digital understanding and literacy: Board members must go beyond a surface-level understanding of digital transformation to guide corporate strategy effectively. This involves actively participating in educational programs, industry briefings, and workshops on emerging technologies, including AI, blockchain, quantum computing, and cybersecurity. Boards should bring in external experts, partner with universities and research institutions, and engage with start-ups to stay informed about current and potential disruptive trends. Additionally, an innovation committee should be established within the board to oversee and drive strategic discussions on technological advancements, ensuring that management is equally committed to fostering innovation throughout the organization.
2. Take calculated risks and promote a calculated risk-taking culture: Boards must shift their mindset from risk avoidance to risk optimization by recognizing that calculated risk-taking is an essential driver of long-term success. This includes establishing a structured framework for evaluating and greenlighting innovative projects, rather than dismissing them due to short-term uncertainties. Directors should actively promote a culture where measured experimentation is encouraged, failures are viewed as learning opportunities, and incremental progress is recognized and rewarded. To reinforce this, companies can develop fail-fast mechanisms, such as innovation sandboxes, where new ideas can be tested with minimal resource investment before being scaled.
3. Create a narrative of innovation: A company's commitment to innovation must be clearly articulated both internally and externally.

Boards should ensure that innovation is not just a corporate buzzword but a tangible, well-communicated, and fully transparent strategy aligning with the company's mission and objectives. This means developing a cohesive innovation narrative that resonates with employees, investors, and customers, highlighting not only breakthrough initiatives but also the company's broader approach to sustained, incremental innovation. Investor updates should emphasize the impact of innovation efforts on long-term value creation, positioning the company as an industry leader rather than a follower reacting to change.

4. Add 30 minutes of innovation to every board meeting: A company that genuinely values innovation must institutionalize, and this begins with boardroom discussions. Setting aside dedicated time in every board meeting for innovation ensures that it is consistently evaluated and prioritized. This segment should go beyond theoretical talks and focus on concrete actions, including reviewing pilot projects, assessing partnerships with start-ups, discussing regulatory challenges related to new technologies, and identifying emerging threats and opportunities. Board members should also engage directly with innovation leaders from within and outside the organization, fostering a cross-functional dialogue that strengthens the company's innovation ecosystem.
5. Incentivize innovation: Innovation should not be an afterthought—it must be embedded into the company's performance evaluation metrics and compensation structures. Board members should oversee the development of KPIs tied to innovation efforts, such as those suggested in this book, ensuring that both senior executives and mid-level managers have a long-term stake interest in innovation success. Instead of solely rewarding short-term financial performance, incentive structures should account for R&D milestones, successful pilot conversions, and ecosystem engagement. By aligning compensation with innovation outcomes, organizations can shift from a risk-averse culture to one that actively encourages bold, forward-thinking initiatives.
6. Diversify the directorate: An overreliance on directors with traditional finance and legal backgrounds limits a board's ability to

navigate the complexities of the digital age. Diversity in expertise, age, and industry experience is crucial for fostering innovative thinking at the highest levels of corporate governance. Boards should proactively recruit directors with diversified backgrounds, including in technology, venture capital, product development, and digital strategy, as well as those of different age groups, different genders, ethnicities, and more. Diversity is critical, and this cannot be stressed enough. By broadening the board's skill set, companies can better anticipate and adapt to disruptive market forces, ensuring that innovation remains a strategic priority.

A fantastic example of innovative leadership can be seen in Accor S.A., a French multinational hospitality company, the largest in Europe and the sixth largest in the world. The company has taken a bold step toward integrating fresh perspectives into its strategic decision-making process by recognizing the importance of engaging younger generations and adapting to a rapidly evolving market. The company created a shadow board—a group of 13 diverse managers, all under 35, representing various regions and expertise areas. These leaders challenge traditional corporate thinking and contribute innovative solutions, directly influencing executive decisions. Their fresh outlooks have already reshaped strategic priorities, such as shifting focus from rigid revenue targets to customer-centric innovation. By collaborating closely with the executive committee, the shadow board ensures that digital-native insights and nontraditional business approaches are incorporated into the company's long-term vision. **The brilliance of this approach is that it provides the company with immense value at no additional cost.**

While the board of directors plays a critical role in setting the strategic direction for innovation, their impact is largely governance-focused, and it is the CEO who truly drives the execution of the agenda. A board that prioritizes innovation is valuable and highly beneficial, but without an engaged and proactive CEO, innovation efforts are likely to remain stagnant. The CEO is the one who must bridge the gap between vision and action.

The most successful CEOs do more than endorse innovation, instead they embed it into the company's culture, decision making, and operational processes. They do so (together with the board) by first **setting a clear and compelling vision for innovation and framing it as a necessity for long-term survival.** CEOs must be transparent and communicate why innovation is essential, ensuring that employees at all levels understand how it ties into the company's growth, efficiency, and market positioning. A company where only R&D teams understand innovation is a company destined to fall behind. When leadership consistently conveys the importance of innovation, it fosters a culture where new ideas are welcomed, and employees feel empowered to think creatively for the good of the company.

Common Open Innovation Pitfalls: Chasing Trends Without Strategic Purpose (Or—"Shiny Object" Syndrome)

Many companies fall into the trap of pursuing emerging technologies, start-ups, or business models without a clear understanding of their relevance to the company's strategic direction and actual value for the company.

Solutions:

- Strategic Relevance Assessment: Always check if an innovation initiative aligns with company goals and market needs before pursuing any innovation initiative.
- Innovation Governance Board: Establish an innovation governance board to prioritize projects based on long-term business impact, not just novelty.
- Strategic Justification: Business units must provide a strategic justification to get funding for new projects and pilots.

Beyond setting the vision, the CEO must take action to remove bureaucratic barriers that hinder innovation. In large corporations, many promising ideas never reach execution because they become entangled in all-too-often slow-moving approval processes, rigid departmental structures, and excessive risk aversion. **An effective CEO ensures that**

innovation teams have the autonomy and resources they need to experiment, iterate, and implement solutions without unnecessary obstacles. This is achieved by fast-tracking pilot programs, allocating dedicated budgets for experimental initiatives, and fostering a culture where calculated risks are encouraged rather than punished.

A CEO committed to open innovation actively engages with external innovation ecosystems, recognizing that the best ideas often do not originate from within the company's walls. CEOs must proactively seek partnerships, attend industry innovation forums, establish corporate accelerators, venture arms, or other similar initiatives that can connect the company with emerging technologies and entrepreneurial talent.

Perhaps the most crucial role of a CEO in this regard is their ability to lead by example. **Employees will not embrace innovation if they see leadership resisting change.** Innovation is always top-down, not bottom-up; that is the simple truth. CEOs must be early adopters of AI-driven decision-making tools, automation, and emerging business models to demonstrate their commitment to technological progress. Whether it's implementing data-driven strategies, experimenting with digital transformation tools, or piloting innovative business models, **CEOs who embrace innovation personally set the tone for the rest of the organization.** When employees witness top leadership actively engaging with new technologies and ideas, they are far more likely to follow suit and integrate innovation into their work.

Like the board, the CEO should ensure alignment between innovation efforts and core business objectives. Successful CEOs ensure that every innovation initiative serves a clear business purpose, whether it enhances customer experience, improves operational efficiency, or generates new revenue streams.

When innovation efforts are not aligned with core business objectives and strategy, they become costly distractions. **Misalignment will lead to wasted resources, increased internal resistance, and initiatives that fail to scale or deliver tangible impact. Worse yet, it causes employees to disengage from innovation altogether, making it more difficult and more expensive to reengage later on.**

One well-known example of misalignment is Google Glass, which serves as an excellent example of the Shiny Object Syndrome.[69] This was a wearable device resembling eyeglasses, equipped with a small transparent display that projected information into the user's field of vision, enabling hands-free interaction with digital content. This innovative product, developed by Google X, failed in the consumer market due to a lack of clear business alignment. While the concept was futuristic, it did not address any pressing customer problems, nor did it align with Google's broader business priorities at the time.

Ultimately, the role of the CEO in open innovation is indispensable. They are not figureheads approving innovation strategies but are the primary drivers who determine whether innovation will succeed. In my experience, there is a significant difference in the success rate of organizations with a strong top-down commitment to innovation compared to those relying solely on bottom-up efforts.

Simply put, innovation doesn't work without top-down buy-in.

---

[69]M. Bulearca and D. Tamarjan, "Augmented Reality: A Sustainable Marketing Tool," *Global Business and Management Research: An International Journal* 2, no. 2 (2010): 237–252.

CHAPTER 18

Overcoming Executive Resistance to Change

The world hates change, yet it is the only thing that has brought progress.

—Charles Kettering

One of the biggest obstacles to open innovation is resistance from senior executives and board members, who often prefer stability over change and disruption.

This resistance is not irrational. Many executives have built their careers by following proven business models and making data-driven, risk-averse decisions. They are measured by short-term financial performance, and their incentives are often tied to quarterly earnings rather than long-term innovation success. Therefore, they believe that they cannot afford to take risks and try new things.

Yet, in a world where technological change is constantly accelerating, staying in your comfort zone is no longer an option. Organizations that fail to adapt will inevitably fall behind. Kodak, Nokia, and Blockbuster are just a few classic, well-known examples of industry giants that once dominated their markets but resisted change, ultimately paying the price. More recently, companies like Thomas Cook and Toys "R" Us have illustrated how even global brands can collapse under the weight of outdated business models.

Thomas Cook, one of the oldest travel companies in the world, founded in 1841, was once considered an icon of the modern travel industry. It pioneered rail-based group tours and later became a leader in global vacation packages and charter flights. At its peak, it served 10 million customers a year and employed over 21,000 people. However, its failure to adapt to the digital age and its continued reliance on phone bookings and physical branches while competitors moved online proved fatal. It struggled with debt, Brexit uncertainty, and changing customer expectations, ultimately ceasing operations in 2019. Despite substantial revenues, the company collapsed under the burden of obsolete infrastructure and a rigid, offline-centric business model.

The downfall of Toys "R" Us follows a similar pattern, where a once undisputed leader in its industry was slow to embrace e-commerce and digital transformation. Instead of investing in a seamless online experience or omnichannel strategies, it relied heavily on big-box stores and seasonal foot traffic. Burdened by massive debt from a leveraged buyout in 2005, it lacked the financial flexibility to innovate. Meanwhile, Amazon, Walmart, and Target adapted quickly to online shopping behaviors and consumer expectations. By the time Toys "R" Us attempted to modernize, it was too late.

In some cases, companies don't shut down entirely but are instead forced into mergers or acquisitions, absorbed by more innovative competitors after failing to keep up with technological progress. Yahoo, Palm, AOL, Compaq, and Blackberry are all examples of such quiet exits that are just as telling as dramatic bankruptcies.

What worked in the past no longer guarantees future success.

Without a culture of innovation, managerial curiosity, and an open door to entrepreneurs and new technologies, corporations risk becoming obsolete. Tomorrow's leaders will be those who proactively adapt and help shape the modern world, not those who cling to past formulas.

Sadly, it is no surprise that many innovation leaders struggle to secure executive buy-in for open innovation initiatives. It is not enough to generate new ideas; these ideas must be implemented at scale, and that, as previously mentioned, requires leadership support.

Before attempting to overcome resistance, it is crucial to understand why executives hesitate to embrace open innovation. While reasons vary, the most common barriers include concerns about cannibalization, short-term financial pressures, lack of technological expertise, and bureaucratic constraints. These are sometimes adjoined with previous endeavors, which, if conducted poorly, can affect the future willingness to commit. I will elaborate a bit on the main barriers, for understanding them is key to reducing them.

One primary reason for executive hesitation is the fear that innovation will disrupt their existing business model. Many leaders worry that investing in new technologies or collaborating with start-ups will undermine their core products and revenue streams. A prime example of this is Kodak, which invented the digital camera but suppressed it because its leadership feared that digital photography would erode its lucrative film business. Instead of leading the transition, Kodak was ultimately disrupted by competitors who embraced the digital future. Turning a blind eye, as you can see, is not a viable strategy, especially in a world where the pace of change is so rapid.

Another major obstacle is short-term pressure. Executives are often measured and rewarded based on quarterly or annual financial results, making them hesitant to invest in long-term, uncertain innovation initiatives. However, in a world where the pace of change is so rapid, failing to adopt innovation can quickly harm the company. Innovation is not a luxury or something relevant only for the long term, it is also critical in the short term. For example, Wix, a leading player in its industry, was recently forced to acquire Base44, a six-month-old, solo-owned, one-man unicorn that had disrupted its business using AI. Similarly, call centers found themselves under existential threat within just one-quarter of 2025, once generative AI technology matured. Many CEOs and board members prioritize predictable revenue streams over high-risk innovation projects that may not show immediate returns.

A lack of technological understanding is another critical issue, as many senior leaders lack backgrounds in emerging technologies and feel uncomfortable making decisions in areas they do not fully comprehend. **Without a solid grasp of innovation trends and disruptive technologies, including AI, executives may hesitate to approve projects they perceive as too complex or risky.**

Bureaucracy presents another challenge. Rigid structures, slow decision-making processes, and multiple layers of approval make it challenging to move quickly on innovation. Internal politics and corporate inertia can delay or even block promising ideas from being implemented. Unlike start-ups, which can pivot and experiment rapidly, large corporations struggle with slow approval processes and internal silos that hinder their ability to test and scale new ideas efficiently.

With that said, despite these challenges, several key strategies can successfully help overcome executive resistance and build leadership buy-in.

One of the most effective ways to gain executive support is to tie innovation directly to business goals. However, it is crucial to recognize that not all innovation initiatives will have immediate, measurable financial outcomes. Some efforts, particularly those focused on long-term transformation or exploratory research, may not have a clear quantitative impact in the short term. **Executives are more likely to champion open innovation when they see a clear link to revenue growth, cost savings, or competitive advantage.** Instead of presenting innovation as an abstract concept, leaders should connect it to specific business objectives, such as expanding into new markets, improving efficiency, or reducing operational costs. Qualitative measures, such as enhanced customer engagement or stronger ecosystem partnerships, should be emphasized for initiatives with less direct financial metrics. Industry benchmarks and competitor examples can be powerful tools to show how leading companies successfully integrate open innovation into their strategy. **Demonstrating how innovation can enhance core business offerings rather than replace them can also help eliminate concerns.**

Another proven approach is to deliver quick wins with pilot programs. Executives often resist large-scale change because it seems too risky, and the benefits appear vague. A more effective approach is to start small and scale gradually. Running small pilot projects to test open innovation initiatives with minimal risk allows organizations to demonstrate early success. Identifying early wins, such as successful collaborations with start-ups or efficiency improvements through technological improvements, such as AI automation, can help build momentum and provide data to support broader adoption.

Educating, training, and involving leadership in the process is another helpful strategy. **Executives are more likely to embrace innovation if they understand the technology and are actively involved in its development**.

Organizations can achieve this by organizing workshops, lectures, and training sessions to improve digital literacy among board members and executives and emphasize the importance of innovation. Inviting leadership to participate in start-up pitch events, hackathons, and other similar activities can help them see new ideas in action. Additionally, pairing executives with innovation mentors who provide insights into emerging technologies and trends can increase their confidence in making informed decisions.

Incentive structures must also be adjusted to reward innovation. Many executives resist innovation because their compensation is tied to short-term financial performance. To encourage risk-taking, companies must introduce long-term performance metrics that reward innovation-driven revenue growth. Executive bonuses should be linked to key innovation KPIs, such as those presented here. Reducing overreliance on short-term, quarterly earnings-based rewards, which discourages investment in long-term innovation, can shift corporate culture toward a more forward-thinking approach.

Overcoming executive resistance is not just about convincing leaders but fundamentally changing how organizations approach innovation. CEOs and board members must lead by example, demonstrating a willingness to embrace change and take calculated risks.

While resistance to change is natural, organizations can no longer afford it. Executives who fail to pick up the mantle of open innovation and champion it, more than risk making their organizations obsolete—they guarantee it.

By learning from the mistakes of companies such as Kodak, organizations can achieve success by tying innovation to business goals, delivering quick wins, educating leadership, and aligning incentives with long-term transformation. This approach enables them to break through resistance and create a culture of innovation, while ensuring they remain relevant.

CHAPTER 19

Demonstrating the Strategic Importance of Open Innovation Across the Organization

Innovation, any new idea, by definition will not be accepted at first. It takes repeated attempts, endless demonstrations, monotonous rehearsals before innovation can be accepted and internalized by an organization.

—Professor Warren G. Bennis

Securing leadership and stakeholder commitment to open innovation is not just about proving its value. Instead, it is about making it impossible to ignore. While executives and board members may acknowledge the theoretical need for innovation, they often struggle to prioritize it in their day-to-day practices.

As stated, executives are often skeptical of change, particularly when it threatens established business models or requires a shift in corporate culture. The most effective way to counter this skepticism is by framing open innovation as an inseparable part of the organization's strategic objectives, a necessity for survival and long-term success, rather than an optional investment.

This means emphasizing not just the potential benefits of open innovation but also the risks of inaction. Leaders should shift the conversation from, "Why should we innovate?" to, "How can we integrate innovation effectively?" When executives understand that open innovation is one of the most efficient ways to strengthen their core business, while guaranteeing growth and resilience, they are far more likely to commit to its success.

Innovation leaders must connect open innovation initiatives to the organization's key business goals to secure leadership support. One classic example of a common business goal is the use of open innovation to optimize efficiency by leveraging external technologies and partnerships that reduce operational expenses. If market expansion is a focus, the conversation should highlight how open innovation enables faster entry into new regions through collaborations or new technologies that serve as enablers.

Demonstrating how industry peers or competitors are utilizing open innovation to drive revenue growth, enhance customer experience, or improve operational resilience can help convey its importance.

I have already acknowledged KPIs as important elements in the successful implementation of open innovation. In this aspect, KPIs can assist innovation leaders in presenting data that link open innovation efforts to concrete business outcomes, including revenue growth, dramatic reduction in R&D costs, time-to-market significant improvements, and more. By consistently measuring and reporting on KPIs, innovation teams can provide executives with the evidence they need to see open innovation as a reliable and strategic investment while ensuring that the rest of the organization understands its importance.

Beyond data, **storytelling plays a crucial role in influencing leadership perception**. Executives as well as other stakeholders are more likely to support open innovation when they can connect with a compelling narrative that explains its importance in the context of the company's journey. Equally important is engaging potential opponents of innovation, the common ones being CISOs and legal departments, through the correct narrative and by involving them directly in pilots and implementations with start-ups relevant to their domains. This hands-on experience can turn skepticism into advocacy and build broader organizational support.

Building a Successful Innovation Narrative

A successful innovation narrative should have the following three key elements:

1. A Clear Threat or Opportunity—Highlighting the competitive pressures, industry disruptions, or emerging trends that make open innovation essential.

2. A Vision for the Future—Depicting how open innovation can position the company as a market leader, enabling it to anticipate and shape future trends rather than react to them.
3. A Practical Path Forward—Providing a concrete plan for how the organization should integrate open innovation into its strategy, including specific initiatives, partnerships, and success metrics.

This narrative should be tailored to different stakeholders within the organization. For board members, the primary focus should be on creating long-term value and mitigating risk. For executives, the emphasis should be on how open innovation aligns with business priorities. For employees, the message should highlight how innovation efforts will create new opportunities and drive companywide growth, emphasizing personal development. Since the rise of generative AI, more employees recognize that failing to integrate technological tools into their daily work risks becoming irrelevant in the job market, making the innovation narrative more personally urgent and easier to highlight. As a reminder, studies show that employees who use AI tools tend to earn between 25[70] and 40 percent[71] more than their colleagues.

Speaking from experience, **a strong indicator that an organization is succeeding in its innovation journey is when managers proactively approach the innovation lead with business challenges**. This shift reflects a growing internal understanding that solutions can and should emerge from innovation initiatives.

In fact, this is one of the most important steps in the innovation journey, and a corporation must be able to accurately define its technological and business challenges in order to know which start-ups it needs to scout for, and what value they are seeking for the collaboration.

Effective communication of open innovation's strategic importance is essential for securing leadership commitment. **Using the correct framing and crafting compelling narratives will enable organizations to**

[70]PwC, "AI Jobs Barometer: How AI Is Reshaping Work and Pay," 2024.
[71]F. Stephany and O. Teutloff, "What Is the Price of a Skill? The Value of Complementarity," *Research Policy* 53, no. 1 (2023): 104898.

overcome executive resistance and drive meaningful change, while ensuring that employees and other stakeholders are engaged and invested in the innovation process.

In the next chapter, I will focus on building organizational engagement beyond your organization's leadership.

CHAPTER 20

Building Organizational Engagement

Great things in business are never done by one person. They're done by a team of people.

—Steve Jobs

In many ways, open innovation is first and foremost about people, and it very much depends on how well an organization engages its employees, fosters a culture of curiosity, and removes internal barriers to collaboration. Without internal buy-in, even the most well-funded innovation strategies will struggle to deliver meaningful impact.

Yet, in many organizations, employees remain disconnected from innovation efforts, as many employees may see innovation as the responsibility of specialized teams rather than as an integral part of their own work. **Overcoming these challenges requires a deliberate effort to embed innovation into the organization's DNA, ensuring that every employee, not just a select few, feels empowered to contribute.**

Organizations that successfully drive open innovation understand that it is not just about collaborating with start-ups or acquiring cutting-edge tools; it requires a curious workforce open to external ideas and willing to experiment. From my experience working with global corporations, I have seen firsthand that companies with an innovation-friendly culture outperform those that resist change. **Without a culture that encourages employees to challenge the status quo and seek new ways of thinking, even the most well-structured innovation strategy will struggle to deliver results.**

Some companies view innovation as an isolated function, confined to R&D or a dedicated innovation department, while **others recognize that innovation must be embedded throughout the organization**.

The latter consistently achieves better results. Curiosity and experimentation must be cultivated intentionally and continuously to build an organization that embraces open innovation.

A fundamental step in fostering a culture of curiosity is creating structured opportunities for employees to explore new ideas and concepts. Many companies I have worked with have implemented internal innovation challenge hackathons, encouraging employees to propose solutions to pressing business challenges. Leadership plays a pivotal role in shaping this culture. I have seen executives in highly innovative organizations engage directly with employees at all levels to discuss new ideas. For instance, a monthly "Ask the CEO" session, where employees could present innovative proposals directly to senior leadership. This not only encourages employees to think outside the box but also signals that innovation is a companywide priority.

Another tool used is embedding experimentation into daily work processes. Employees should be encouraged to test and iterate on their ideas in small, low-risk ways.

One of the most significant barriers I've observed in large organizations is the fear of failure. Employees hesitate to propose new ideas because they fear rejection, criticism, or even repercussions if their ideas do not succeed. Organizations must actively counter this mindset by fostering a culture where failure is seen as a necessary part of learning. A "fail-fast, learn-faster" approach,[72] where employees are encouraged to take calculated risks and quickly iterate based on feedback, is essential. While this may seem like internal innovation, it is also done to build a cultural foundation for the success of open innovation. **Without a supportive environment that tolerates risk and embraces learning, collaboration with external partners will often stall or fail.**

Some companies successfully mitigate this fear by celebrating "lessons learned" from failed projects on a quarterly basis, including external collaboration projects. By reframing failure as a valuable learning experience, employees became more willing to experiment, collaborate externally, and

[72]N. Koporcic, D. Sjödin, M. Kohtamäki, & V. Parida, "Embracing the 'Fail Fast and Learn Fast' Mindset: Conceptualizing Learning from Failure in Knowledge-Intensive SMEs," *Small Business Economics* 64, no. 1 (2025): 181–202.

integrate new ideas from outside the organization. In this way, **a strong internal culture of innovation becomes the enabler of effective open innovation.**

Organizations must also provide employees with continuous exposure to external ideas to sustain curiosity and innovation. This goes beyond just partnerships. Encouraging employees to attend conferences, participate in industry roundtables, or work temporarily with start-ups provides them with fresh perspectives. Some companies take it a step further by implementing "reverse mentoring" programs, where younger, digitally native employees coach senior executives on emerging trends and technologies. This has proven particularly effective in keeping leadership engaged with technological advancements.

Knowledge sharing must also become an integral part of the company's innovation strategy. Employees who engage with new ideas externally should be encouraged to share those insights with the organization. Companies can create formalized learning networks where employees present insights gained from conferences, start-up collaborations, or industry research. For example, a "Lunch & Learn" series, where employees from different departments could share insights from recent events or projects. Additionally, a chat group for employees with an innovation orientation can foster engagement and openness, enabling any employee who encounters a challenge or a potential solution to share it instantly. Such simple initiatives can create a ripple effect, sparking new conversations and cross-departmental collaboration.

As previously stated, bureaucracy is a major obstacle to fostering curiosity and innovation; employees should not feel compelled to navigate layers of red tape to test a new idea. Organizations should streamline their decision-making processes to enable quick experimentation, not only to facilitate effective innovation but also to foster a culture that promotes experimentation. One effective approach is to ensure that the company conducts cross-functional innovation workshops, which are not limited to business units but also include corporate functions such as legal, regulatory, procurement, and finance.

At the same time, not all employees naturally embrace curiosity, and some may actively resist change. Employees who have spent years perfecting a particular process or business model often feel threatened by new approaches. They may perceive curiosity as inefficient or view external ideas as distractions from their core responsibilities.

Organizations must frame innovation as a job enabler, not as a job threat, if they are to engage these employees. **Employees are more likely to support change if they understand how new approaches can make their work easier or more impactful.** For example, AI-driven automation can eliminate repetitive tasks, enabling employees to focus on the more creative aspects of their work.

Generative AI, which will be discussed in further detail later, plays a crucial role in this process, as it helps engage employees by making them realize that technology is not only vital to their company but also essential for their own career development. It shifts their perspective from seeing technology adoption, whether AI or other innovations, as merely benefiting the organization to recognizing how it enhances their position in the organization and the job market. In the past, engagement was often driven by fear regarding what would happen to the organization and its employees if they failed to adopt new technologies. Since the rise of generative AI, more employees have come to understand that although it is just one tool, it has helped open minds to broader technological adoption, increasing their willingness to embrace innovation as a whole. Organizations and corporate leaders must recognize that generative AI is just one of many relevant technologies, and they should not become overly fixated on this single solution. True innovation requires a holistic approach that incorporates multiple technological advancements, rather than relying solely on one.

Incentives, as mentioned before, play a critical role in shaping behavior. If employees see that innovation is rewarded, they will be more likely to embrace it. This is true for managers, and it is true for any other employee. Organizations should recognize and celebrate employees who challenge conventional thinking through formal awards, promotions, or financial incentives, preferably with visibility at companywide meetings or platforms. **Measuring success solely by a quarterly profit-and-loss report is destructive for middle and long-term strategy.**

Employees can also be paired with innovation mentors, connecting skeptical employees with innovation champions, while creating structured learning opportunities that turn curiosity into a personal growth opportunity rather than an imposed requirement.

Companies can also gamify innovation participation, for example, by introducing internal innovation leaderboards, competitions, and reward systems to encourage even hesitant employees to contribute ideas.

It is essential to highlight that while leadership plays a critical role in shaping innovation culture, **middle managers are often the gatekeepers who determine whether curiosity and experimentation thrive or are stifled.** If mid-level managers prioritize efficiency and short-term KPIs over learning and experimentation, employees will feel discouraged from exploring new ideas. To ensure that middle management fosters curiosity rather than obstructing it, organizations should similarly incentivize managers to support innovation, train managers to coach curiosity and facilitate brainstorming sessions, while providing constructive feedback and recognizing innovative managers.

A key lesson from leading innovators is that curiosity is contagious. When employees see their peers, including middle and C-level management, as well as colleagues across departments, innovating and benefiting from innovation, they are more likely to adopt an open mindset and pursue innovation themselves. This stands in contrast to the NIH mentality I described earlier, where employees resist external ideas and block initiatives. By fostering visible curiosity and cross-departmental engagement, organizations can actively counteract NIH and replace it with a culture of openness and shared learning.

Encouraging an innovative mindset requires consistent effort, investment, and a willingness to challenge entrenched ways of thinking. Companies that succeed in this transformation will not only enhance their internal innovation capabilities but will also become far more effective in external open innovation efforts. An organization's ability to partner with the best and brightest external innovators will always be limited by its ability to foster curiosity, openness, and experimentation within its workforce. By embedding these values into the company's culture, organizations can create a dynamic environment where employees are empowered to explore, experiment, and drive meaningful change.

One meaningful way to successfully invest in building internal capabilities is through training. Innovation requires more than just having the right ideas or the right culture; it necessitates having the right people with the right skills, the right mindset, and the right tools to bring ideas to life.

Organizations that invest in training and development for their employees create innovation-ready teams that can actively participate in open innovation, collaborate effectively with external partners, and rapidly integrate new technologies and methodologies into their workflows. Similar to other out-of-the-day-to-day initiatives, when people are well-trained, aligned, and motivated, results from innovation processes improve dramatically. **Innovation requires more than good ideas and partnerships; it requires a strong foundation and continuous internal readiness.**

Throughout my career, I have had the pleasure of working with numerous corporations across industries, helping them navigate the complexities of open innovation, digital transformation, and technological disruption. One of the biggest challenges I have observed is that while many organizations recognize the need to innovate, they often lack the practical skills to effectively engage with external innovation ecosystems. This is where structured training programs, workshops, and lectures become critical, as they serve as catalysts for change, equipping employees and leadership teams with the tools and frameworks necessary to drive innovation forward.

Without structured training, education, and skill development, employees, from the very top to the bottom of the corporate ladder, may struggle to engage meaningfully in innovation efforts. Innovation cannot be expected to happen spontaneously, and organizations should actively equip their workforce, particularly C-level and mid-level management, with the tools and knowledge they need to thrive and innovate in a modern world.

One barrier to open innovation is the skills gap that currently exists within organizations. Many employees, in relevant positions, lack the technical, creative, or strategic skills required to identify new opportunities, evaluate disruptive technologies, or effectively collaborate with external innovators. Therefore, companies must use structured training programs that provide employees with hands-on experience, real-world problem-solving, and exposure to cutting-edge technologies and methodologies.

This requires organizations to evaluate the skills needed to succeed and diagnose existing opportunity gaps. It also requires using the right methodologies to build missing or lacking capabilities, particularly in areas such as design thinking, digital literacy, agile development, external collaboration, and working with new technologies. This might also require going much further than reskilling individuals and might instead require significant changes within the company.

Innovation training should be immersive and experiential, and traditional corporate training, such as passive e-learning modules, will not be sufficient for an innovative mindset shift. Instead, the most successful companies implement active, real-world learning experiences that develop innovation skills in practice. A comprehensive training framework should include some of the following elements:

- Workshops on Design Thinking and Problem-Solving: Design thinking is a human-centered approach to innovation that helps employees challenge assumptions, redefine problems, and solve problems creatively.
- Agile and Lean Start-Up Training: Projects often follow rigid, top-down planning processes in traditional corporate environments. However, in open innovation, flexibility and rapid iteration are essential. Organizations should train employees in agile methodologies, helping them adopt a test-and-learn mindset.
- Corporate–Start-Up Exchange Programs and Meetups: One of the most effective ways to develop innovation skills is through direct exposure to start-up environments. Some corporations temporarily assign employees to start-ups or venture accelerators, allowing them to gain firsthand insight into entrepreneurial thinking, rapid execution, and external collaboration. At the same time, even regular meetings and demo days with start-ups can greatly benefit employees.
- Innovation Sprints and Internal Hackathons: Many successful companies host regular internal hackathons where employees across departments collaborate to solve pressing business challenges. These events foster creative problem-solving, encourage interdisciplinary teamwork, and expose employees to new technologies and ways of doing things. Unlike traditional brainstorming meetings, hackathons focus on building tangible prototypes within a short time frame, driving real innovation impact.

- Disruptive Technologies Training for All Employees: Given the rapid technological advancement, particularly in AI and GenAI, all employees—and not just IT teams—must understand how these technologies impact their roles. Companies should launch companywide sessions and programs, including AI literacy initiatives, to ensure that employees at every level can effectively leverage these tools to enhance productivity and informed decision making. This includes hands-on training with generative AI, automation software, and data analytics platforms.
- Partnerships with Universities and Online Learning Platforms: Corporations can partner with academic institutions and edtech platforms to offer specialized innovation courses. Some companies even sponsor employees to complete professional certifications in innovation management, digital transformation, and entrepreneurship.

While there are many applicable methodologies in the market, such as design thinking workshops, Agile and Lean start-up training, start-up exchange programs, hackathons, and disruptive technology sessions, the most effective training I have developed is my proprietary innovation workshop methodology. This is not just another tool but a proven, results-driven system that works across industries and organizational structures. It must be placed at the forefront of any innovation training strategy.

In each unit of the organization, including C-level executives, the board, and every division, I lead a hands-on innovation workshop that begins with a powerful, engaging lecture. Then, from a curated database of over 50 relevant start-ups, we select 10 that provide real solutions to three to five strategic challenges raised by that specific team. These workshops consistently produce immediate results, including, on average, seven follow-up meetings with start-ups and one to two pilots per workshop. This cross-organizational approach ensures alignment, creates measurable outcomes, and delivers innovation both at scale and quickly.

This is not theory. This is a method that works.

Lectures and executive training play a key role in driving innovation. When I speak at corporate events and global conferences, I focus on breaking down complex innovation challenges into actionable strategies, helping leadership teams see the direct link between innovation and business success. **One of the biggest mistakes I see in corporate settings is leaders expecting innovation to happen organically, without investing in proper training, resources, or cultural shifts.** Through my lectures, I aim to bridge that gap, providing executives with the insights and frameworks they need to champion open innovation within their organizations.

Ultimately, training and development are not just about acquiring new skills but also about changing mindsets and embedding innovation into the company's DNA. I have seen firsthand how companies that invest in ongoing learning initiatives, hands-on workshops, and executive training are the ones that stay ahead of the curve, attract top talent, and continuously reinvent themselves.

Organizations should understand that innovation training is not a one-time initiative but rather a continuous part of corporate culture and a long-term commitment. The most successful companies treat innovation training as a constant, evolving process rather than a fixed curriculum. Choosing the teams participating in training is essential and can be done accurately when innovation is aligned with strategic goals. For example, the business teams that are crucial to the organization's success are those that should be part of acquiring an innovative skill set. Organizations that fail to do so and fail to equip their employees with the right skills and tools will struggle to continue and remain competitive.

By implementing hands-on training, real-world innovation experiences, and structured learning programs, companies can futureproof their workforce and ensure that their teams are not just ready for change but actively driving it. At the same time, by providing employees and leaders with the right tools and frameworks, organizations can also turn open innovation from an abstract concept into a practical, results-driven strategy that fuels long-term success.

Implementing this suggested approach will quickly turn open innovation from an abstract concept into a practical, results-driven strategy that delivers measurable impact for your organization.

CHAPTER 21

Encouraging Cross-Departmental Collaboration

Coming together is a beginning. Keeping together is progress. Working together is success.

—Henry Ford

While external collaboration with start-ups and technology partners is essential, internal collaboration within an organization is just as critical. Unfortunately, many companies suffer from rigid silos, where departments function as separate entities, each focusing on its own objectives with little regard for cross-functional alignment. This siloed approach stifles innovation, slows down decision making, and creates inefficiencies that put organizations at a competitive disadvantage.

To drive open innovation successfully, companies must break down internal silos and foster a culture of shared knowledge, teamwork, and transparency. This means not only creating formal mechanisms for collaboration but also reshaping the company's mindset to prioritize collective success over individual departmental achievements. Innovation thrives when employees from various departments, including R&D, marketing, sales, IT, legal, finance, and operations, collaborate to solve problems, explore new opportunities, and challenge conventional thinking. Innovation collaboration processes sometimes create another advantage for organizations: Shifting political and noncollaborative organizations to those who enjoy the benefits of a healthy collaborative culture, by incentivizing employees to cooperate. At the same time, it allows and promotes external collaboration.

Simply put: You are more open to external collaboration when you do not focus on internal politics.

How to Foster Cross-Departmental Engagement

The following practical steps can help organizations foster cross-departmental engagement:

1. Organizations should form specialized teams, empowered with resources and authority, with members from different departments to tackle specific innovation challenges or pilot new initiatives.
2. Organizations should allow employees to spend time in different departments to develop a more holistic understanding of the company, its challenges, and the opportunities ahead.
3. Companies should align performance metrics across teams so that collaboration is not seen as an additional task but as a responsibility tied to business success.

Building a collaborative, innovation-driven culture requires strategic thinking and planning. One of the most effective ways to break down silos is to create structured opportunities for collaboration. While spontaneous teamwork is valuable, companies that systematize cross-departmental interaction will see much stronger and more sustainable results.

These structures ensure that collaboration is not just a one-time initiative but an integral part of the company's operations.

One significant barrier to effective cross-departmental collaboration is a lack of shared tools and communication channels. Companies often use different systems for various departments, resulting in fragmented workflows and hindering collaboration. Companies should instead invest in cross-departmental collaborative platforms that allow for real-time communication and project management. Organizations should also create internal knowledge-sharing platforms, such as internal Wikipedia pages or AI-driven knowledge bases, to share knowledge and insight across teams. AI can also be used to connect with the right people within the organization, allowing for better cross-departmental collaboration.

It is important to understand that while frameworks and technology can facilitate collaboration, leadership ultimately determines success.

If executives and managers continue to reinforce siloed thinking, efforts to foster collaboration will fail. This is why leadership should actively engage with different departments, participate in cross-functional meetings, and demonstrate a commitment to collaborative decision making, while also promoting transparency and working to eliminate internal politics, which often serves as the greatest barrier to collaboration. **Leadership must create a culture where departments view each other as partners rather than rivals.**

While cross-functional collaboration has significant benefits, organizations often encounter challenges that undermine their efforts. Recognizing and addressing these issues early can make all the difference and help build the foundations for organizations to succeed in open innovation.

One key challenge in fostering cross-departmental collaboration is the lack of clearly defined goals. **Too often, companies push for collaboration without outlining specific objectives**, leading to unfocused discussions and projects that fail to generate meaningful outcomes. When teams are unclear about the purpose and expected results of their collaboration, their efforts can become fragmented and misaligned with broader business goals. **To ensure productive collaboration, leadership must articulate clear, measurable objectives that guide cross-functional teams toward tangible results**. Defining success criteria from the outset helps employees understand the value of their contributions and keeps efforts focused on achieving real impact.

Common Open Innovation Pitfalls: Poor Integration Between Innovation Teams and Core Business Units

Innovation efforts often fail when treated as separate functions rather than integrated into the company's core business.

Solutions:

- Develop a Cross-Functional Innovation Team structure, ensuring that innovation is embedded within business units and that employees from different departments work together.

- Require innovation teams to codevelop solutions with business-unit leaders, ensuring that the end users and unit leaders are involved in shaping the solutions from the start.
- Implement initiatives while outlining a clear process for transitioning successful pilot projects into fully operational and scaled-up projects and solutions.

Another common pitfall is an excessive number of meetings with too little action. I am sure you, the reader, have seen this in your organization. Collaboration often turns into lengthy, unfocused discussions rather than decision making and execution, distracting from what needs to be done. The most crucial goal of joint meetings should be problem-solving—a clear drive toward practical, implementable solutions. Meetings should always serve a purpose—whether problem-solving, decision making, or strategic alignment, and companies should foster a culture of concise, well-structured, and outcome-driven meetings. Setting clear agendas, assigning action items, and following up with accountability measures ensure that meetings drive progress and improve productivity.

A lack of incentives is another issue; employees naturally prioritize tasks tied to their individual performance metrics. Collaboration will always be considered secondary if it is not explicitly linked to performance evaluations and rewards. Organizations should integrate cross-functional collaboration into their incentive structures, ensuring that employees see it as an integral part of their roles rather than an extra responsibility. Recognition programs, financial incentives, and career development opportunities for those who excel in collaborative efforts can reinforce the importance of teamwork across departments.

To overcome the barriers to collaboration, organizations must take deliberate steps to streamline decision making, provide tangible incentives for cross-functional teamwork, and invest in the right technology to support collaboration without adding bureaucratic overhead. By eliminating inefficiencies and ensuring that collaboration is purposeful, companies can transform their internal structures to be more agile, innovative, and adaptable to changing market conditions.

Ongoing training and development sessions, such as previously mentioned, can further solidify collaborative efforts. Employees need to be equipped with the skills to navigate cross-departmental dynamics effectively. Workshops on innovation, communication, conflict resolution, and interdisciplinary problem-solving can help break down resistance and enable smoother team interactions. Additionally, leadership training programs that emphasize the role of managers in fostering collaboration can ensure that companywide initiatives receive top-down support.

For organizations to remain competitive in the evolving business landscape, internal collaboration must become a strategic priority rather than an afterthought. Companies can unlock new levels of innovation and efficiency by following the suggested tips, implementing structured collaboration frameworks, leveraging the right technology, and fostering a leadership-driven culture of transparency and shared success.

CHAPTER 22

The Head of Innovation as the Architect of Change and Collaboration

CIOs are in a unique position where they have a full view of the business and are using their understanding to drive transformation.

—Anjali Shaikh

For open innovation to succeed, it cannot exist as an abstract concept or a series of disconnected initiatives. Open innovation requires a dedicated leader to drive execution, foster alignment, and embed innovation into the company's DNA. This critical role is that of the head of innovation.

Heads of innovation are not just decorated project managers as some might think; instead, they are change agents, turning open innovation from a concept into a core business function, critical not only for advancing open innovation but also for securing the company's future. Selecting the right head of innovation is one of the most critical decisions a company can make in its open innovation journey. Choosing the wrong fit can lead to delayed execution, lack of organizational alignment, or failure to scale innovation beyond isolated projects. Since time is the scarcest resource, such situations must be avoided at all costs.

Equally important is the decision regarding who this person reports to; whether directly to the CEO, to the CTO, the chief strategy officer, or another executive leader. This reporting line has a significant impact on the innovation leader's ability to influence the organization and align innovation with broader strategic priorities and should be carefully considered in any innovation strategy.

Some companies assume that innovation can be managed as a side project, distributed across existing leadership roles. Others believe hiring an external expert with connections to the start-up ecosystem is the best way to accelerate open innovation. However, my extensive experience in this area shows that, in most cases, the most effective heads of innovation come from within the organization itself, and this is what I always advise CEOs who call me to ask if I can recommend an external hire.

Compared to an external hire, an internal hire brings several advantages: they already possess deep organizational knowledge, understand corporate culture and informal power dynamics, and enjoy established trust and influence across departments. This enables faster execution, smoother navigation of approvals, and better alignment with company strategy. Internal hires are better equipped to drive change while managing resistance, work effectively across silos, and are well-versed in compliance and regulatory requirements. They are more likely to demonstrate long-term commitment, ensuring continuity in innovation efforts.

This is why an internal hire is almost always the preferred option, being more effective at navigating the corporate structure, securing buy-in, and driving execution. External hires should only be considered when there is no suitable internal candidate available. While external hires may bring fresh thinking and knowledge of the external ecosystem, this knowledge gap can be bridged through the support of external advisers or consultants. The reverse, instilling organizational trust, cultural fluency, and internal influence, is significantly harder to achieve through an external appointment. The right choice depends on the company's priorities, current innovation culture, and level of internal resistance. Still, organizations should treat internal promotion as the default path, with external consultants providing support as needed. This structure ensures the company has a leader who knows how to get things done internally while remaining connected to external opportunities, which is perhaps the most significant challenge in innovation.

To make this hybrid approach work, organizations should:

1. Pair the head of innovation with external partners. This could be an external consultant or advisory board, including start-up founders, investors, and industry experts.
2. Provide the head of innovation with opportunities to participate in external innovation events, accelerators, and start-up meetups to connect with new ideas and business models.

3. Build an internal innovation team that includes members with external experience, to balance corporate knowledge with outside thinking.

By taking this approach, companies can maintain internal alignment while ensuring that innovation efforts are informed by the latest developments in the external ecosystem.

The head of innovation must possess two critical traits:

1. Exceptional Project Management Skills—Open innovation involves multiple stakeholders, tight deadlines, and cross-functional execution. The head of innovation must be the best project manager in the organization, ensuring that initiatives move from idea to implementation without getting stuck in corporate inertia.
2. Strong People Skills and Organizational Influence—The head of innovation is not just responsible for processes; they must engage, inspire, and align people across the organization. They must build trust, navigate resistance, and ensure that external start-ups and partners are considered strategic allies rather than threats.

The best heads of innovation carry something rare; a combination of ingenuity, courage (Or "Chutzpah" if you will), and strategic fluency. These qualities often distinguish between a stalled initiative and a breakthrough moment.

Ingenuity enables heads of innovation to revive start-up collaborations that seemed dead, reconfigure deals that have flatlined, and find alternative routes when primary ones are blocked. Heads of innovation often champion solutions that challenge the status quo.

Courage means knowing when to challenge internal assumptions, pushing back on unrealistic demands, and walking away from opportunities that will not land. Navigating the nuances of different organizational cultures and even international sensitivities requires a sharp instinct and thick skin. Sometimes, it means taking a bold bet, such as requesting a budget during a freeze, because the payoff justifies the risk.

Ultimately, strategic fluency stems from combining a broad perspective with in-depth expertise. Great innovation leaders do not need legal expertise, nor do they have to be engineers. Still, they must know enough to ask the right questions, negotiate compromises, and draw from a catalog of start-ups and trends.

To revisit the earlier discussion on the role of consultancies, it is essential to highlight a fundamental distinction that underscores a core limitation compared to heads of innovation. In my experience, strategic consultancies almost always operate with delayed visibility into the most disruptive technologies. In contrast, experienced corporate heads of innovation are embedded in entrepreneurial ecosystems and, therefore, are rarely, if ever, caught off guard by disruptive technologies.

While strategy consulting firms may only detect innovative solutions once a start-up has built a digital footprint, launched a product, raised capital, or made headlines, a well-connected innovation leader often hears about it first, long before public awareness. This is because the most promising entrepreneurs, often still working in stealth mode, seek advice and validation from corporate leaders they respect. These conversations occur below the radar, without the need for pitch decks or press releases.

This early access allows innovation leaders to respond and shape outcomes. When a corporation learns about game-changing technologies before the market does, it can act decisively: invest early, form exclusive partnerships, or be the first to integrate a solution that others will not be aware of until it may be too late. Consider, for example, a banking corporation that identifies an AI-driven solution capable of replacing 80 percent of its bankers with digital agents. If it acts swiftly, secures exclusive deployment rights, and scales the technology before competitors know of its existence, it will likely result in dominance. This is the power of seeing the future before your competitors even know where to look, and it is a strategic advantage that is rarely achieved through traditional consulting firms. It is only likely to result from the work of an experienced and talented head of innovation.

Likewise, as previously mentioned, the reporting line of the head of innovation is not merely an organizational formality but also a strategic decision that significantly influences the success of open innovation initiatives. In many organizations, innovation is mistakenly placed under R&D or IT, limiting its scope and reducing its role to one related only to technological advancements or product development. However, open innovation transcends any single department. It touches strategy, operations, partnerships, culture, and customer experience. Therefore, the head of innovation should report directly to a senior and powerful executive who has a broad, cross-functional mandate: typically, the CEO, the chief strategy officer, or in some cases, the COO. This positioning signals to the rest of the organization that innovation is a core strategic priority, not a support function.

Reporting to the CEO or CSO empowers the head of innovation to break down silos, align innovation initiatives with long-term business goals, and secure buy-in from other C-level executives. It ensures that innovation is considered during strategic planning and that resources, attention, and authority are allocated accordingly.

To truly embed innovation into the company's DNA and enable cross-departmental collaboration, the innovation leader must operate at the highest level of the organization, with a clear mandate to drive change and access to decision makers across all business units. This structural clarity is a prerequisite for innovation to scale, sustain, and deliver measurable business value.

To assess your company's readiness for open innovation, ask yourself these questions:

1. Who in our organization is accountable for making open innovation work?
2. Do we have a head of innovation with the authority and execution ability to drive change?
3. Are we setting this role up for success with the right resources, executive backing, and external support?

Innovation requires a leader who knows how to bring it to life. Organizations that invest in empowering the right head of innovation are setting themselves for success.

CHAPTER 23

Tackling Barriers and Resistance

You can't allow tradition to get in the way of innovation. There's a need to respect the past, but it's a mistake to revere your past."

—Bob Iger

Innovation is often seen as solely an external challenge—finding the right technologies, forming the right partnerships, and staying ahead of the competition. However, as previously mentioned, **some of the most significant obstacles to innovation come from within the organization itself**. Resistance to change, rigid hierarchies, bureaucratic inefficiencies, and fear of failure can quietly bring even the most promising efforts to an unsuccessful end. Without addressing these internal barriers, even the most well-funded and well-intentioned innovation strategies will struggle to gain traction.

From frontline staff to senior executives, employees may hesitate to take risks, fearing failure or disruption to established workflows. At the same time, internal policies, budgetary constraints, and a lack of alignment between different departments can create an environment where innovation is seen as an added burden rather than the strategic necessity that it is.

To remain competitive, organizations must take deliberate steps to ensure that innovation efforts will succeed. This chapter dives deep into the previously mentioned barriers. It examines the structural, cultural, and psychological barriers that hinder innovation within large organizations, while providing practical tools to overcome them. Here, I will present the fear of failure and resistance to change that hold employees and leaders back, as well as the bureaucratic and operational blockers that prevent innovation. Additionally, I will discuss the best ways to manage uncertainty when engaging in transformative projects.

By addressing these internal challenges and breaking down these barriers, organizations can ensure they are well prepared to innovate successfully and stay ahead of the curve.

Successful innovation demands an environment where ideas can take root, develop, and thrive. **No matter how much a company invests in innovation or external partnerships, if its people resist change and its culture does not support it, true innovation will never take hold**.

As previously mentioned, employees, especially those working for large, traditional, and risk-averse organizations, often worry that suggesting new ideas or experimenting with new approaches could backfire, harming their reputation or career prospects. I have seen this fear paralyze talented professionals with great ideas. To counter this, **companies must reframe failure as a learning opportunity rather than a career-ending mistake**. One effective method is through the "Lessons Learned" framework, where employees who have worked on unsuccessful projects share their experiences with colleagues to discuss key takeaways and prevent the same mistakes from happening again. Rewarding employees for identifying what does not work, rather than punishing them, is another crucial step toward tackling this barrier to innovation.

Hierarchical corporate structures also pose a major cultural and psychological barrier. I have worked with companies where junior employees struggled to make their voices heard due to rigid management layers. In such organizations, the fear of disrupting established chains of command discourages employees from challenging the status quo. Companies must foster a culture where input from all levels is valued, rather than stifled. Organizations can encourage a more open dialogue around innovation by ensuring leadership is approachable and transparent and by creating forums where employees can share insights without fear of reprimand.

Another major cultural roadblock is risk aversion. Many organizations, especially in highly regulated industries, prioritize stability over experimentation. While compliance is essential, an overly cautious mindset can prevent necessary adaptation and growth. Encouraging a mindset shift from risk avoidance to calculated risk-taking is key. Leaders should actively promote pilot programs and small-scale testing environments where employees can experiment with new ideas without fear of widespread failure.

Misaligned incentives can further discourage employees from pursuing innovation. If employees are primarily evaluated based on efficiency and short-term results, they will naturally deprioritize long-term, innovative projects with inherent uncertainty. To address this, organizations should incorporate innovation-based performance metrics into employee evaluations. Using these metrics, organizations should reward those who generate successful ideas and recognize contributions toward experimentation and learning. Incentivizing cross-functional collaboration and participation in pilot programs can further reinforce an innovation-friendly culture.

To create an organization that truly embraces innovation, leaders must go beyond encouraging creative thinking. They must actively remove the psychological and cultural barriers that prevent it. This means establishing a culture where failure is viewed as an opportunity for learning, hierarchies do not suppress valuable insights, risk-taking is encouraged, and incentives are aligned with long-term growth rather than short-term efficiency. Organizations that take these steps will not only generate more ideas but also build the foundations that will enable them to turn ideas into tangible business results.

At the same time, while cultural and psychological barriers hinder innovation at an individual level, systemic obstacles embedded in corporate structures often present even greater challenges.

Excessive bureaucracy, rigid approval processes, and resource misallocation can prematurely end innovation before it can even truly begin. Many organizations fall into the trap of maintaining outdated procedures, where innovative ideas must navigate endless meetings, documentation, and approval layers. Even when employees are encouraged to think creatively, structural inefficiencies and resource constraints can drain the momentum of innovation and prevent ideas from ever becoming a reality.

To create an environment where innovation is not just encouraged but is implemented, companies must take deliberate steps to eliminate unnecessary procedural roadblocks and optimize resource allocation. Here, I will detail some of the most common systemic barriers to innovation and offer concrete solutions to overcome them.

Bureaucratic Gridlock: Bureaucracy serves a vital function in large organizations, ensuring governance, compliance, and risk management.

However, when approval processes become too rigid or complex, they slow decision making to a crawl and stop innovative ideas from getting past the proposal stage. To reduce bureaucratic friction, organizations can:

- Simplify Approval Frameworks: Instead of requiring multiple layers of signoffs for every initiative, organizations can implement decision-making matrixes to clarify roles and ensure that only essential stakeholders are involved.
- Empower Autonomous Innovation Teams: Organizations should establish cross-functional teams with the authority to decide on pilot projects without going through traditional executive review. These teams should have preapproved budgets and clear guidelines on when leadership input is required.
- Create "Fast-Track" Innovation Pathways: Certain projects, such as those aligned with strategic goals or requiring minimal investment, should qualify for expedited approval. Dedicated "innovation champions" within leadership can serve as sponsors to remove roadblocks for high-potential initiatives, while working with the head of innovation. The most successful heads of innovation will have many such champions, with whom they will be able to work on different initiatives.
- Reduce Internal Red Tape: Many bureaucratic barriers exist not due to regulatory requirements but because of outdated internal policies. Organizations should regularly audit their processes to eliminate unnecessary steps.

Companies can ensure that promising ideas are not buried under procedural inertia by making decision making more agile and empowering teams to act quickly.

Unoptimized Resource Allocation for Innovation: Even when bureaucratic hurdles are reduced, innovation cannot thrive without dedicated resources. In some cases, organizations treat innovation as a secondary priority, funding it only after operational needs are met. This reactive approach leads to underfunded initiatives that fail before they gain traction. To address this, companies must proactively allocate time, funding, and expertise to support long-term innovation. These are some of the steps that organizations can take to do so:

- Establish Dedicated Innovation Budgets: Rather than relying solely on departments to fund innovation from their operational budgets, companies should create separate funding streams for experimentation and pilot projects, particularly those related to cross-departmental collaboration. These budgets should be protected from short-term cost-cutting pressures.
- Requiring In-Departmental Innovation Budget: Beyond the separate budget, departments must also be forced to use some of their own budgets. This will allow for better harnessing of department managers for the innovation process.
- Adopt a Portfolio Approach to Innovation Investments: Just as financial investors diversify their portfolios, companies should spread investment across low-risk incremental innovations and high-risk, high-reward breakthrough ideas, often through a large number of pilots. This ensures that even in resource-limited environments, innovation remains a priority.
- Encourage Cross-Department Collaboration: Instead of each department competing for innovation funding, organizations can establish centralized innovation hubs that provide shared access to expertise, technology, and infrastructure, while allowing people from different departments to come together and innovate collaboratively.
- Leverage External Partnerships: Start-ups, universities, and research institutions can offer cutting-edge solutions without requiring massive internal investments. Companies should actively engage in codevelopment initiatives, accelerator programs, and conduct pilots with ecosystem players to expand their capabilities.
- Allow Employees Time to Innovate: Employees often lack the bandwidth to pursue new ideas amid their day-to-day responsibilities. Google's famous "20% time" model, where employees dedicate a portion of their work hours to side projects, has led to significant innovations. Organizations should consider similar initiatives that allow employees to contribute to innovation

without jeopardizing their core responsibilities. Noting that Google has utilized this approach for internal innovation, I suggest that organizations allocate some of this time to focus on different challenges and improvements that can be made through collaboration.

- Implement ROI-Driven Prioritization: Not all ideas merit the same level of investment. Companies can adopt a model where projects must meet specific performance milestones, according to different preagreed KPIs, before receiving additional funding. This ensures that resources are allocated efficiently to the most promising initiatives.

By taking a structured approach to resource allocation, companies can avoid the pitfall of treating innovation as an afterthought and instead make it a sustainable, long-term capability. **Organizations must understand that overcoming systemic barriers to innovation requires more than one-off process changes.** To truly do so, organizations must fundamentally shift their approach to decision making, resource allocation, and organizational structure.

CHAPTER 24

Measuring Success in Open Innovation

Measurement is the first step that leads to control and eventually to improvement. If you can't measure something, you can't understand it. If you can't understand it, you can't control it. If you can't control it, you can't improve it.

—H. James Harrington

Organizations that embrace open innovation often ask a critical question: How do we measure success? Unlike traditional R&D, where internal processes and outcomes are easier to track, open innovation involves multiple external stakeholders, shifting priorities, and long-term impact that are often not immediately visible. **Without clear performance metrics, even the most ambitious open innovation strategies can struggle to demonstrate value and even fail entirely.** Additionally, traditional managers will find it challenging to commit without a proven measure of success.

It should therefore come as no surprise that **while the majority of corporate leaders today acknowledge the importance of innovation, many struggle with the challenge of how to properly measure innovation and "prove" its impact.**

There are different approaches to measuring innovation, and while different methods may examine innovation differently, it is of key importance that organizations have a clear, structured methodology by which they can measure whether or not their innovation efforts are bearing fruit.

Organizations that fail to track and analyze their open innovation efforts risk investing in projects that never translate into tangible business outcomes. However, innovation measurement is notoriously complex, and many traditional business metrics do not account for the unique nature of innovation, where progress is often nonlinear. Success may come in forms other than immediate financial returns.

For open innovation to thrive, companies must establish clear KPIs that track the effectiveness of their initiatives. These KPIs should assess leadership engagement, process efficiency, collaboration outcomes, financial impact, and the ability to scale successful projects. They should also account for qualitative factors, such as cultural shifts and employee engagement, that contribute to long-term innovation success.

One of the most effective ways to measure open innovation is through pilots which serve as small-scale implementations that test new technologies, business models, or partnerships before full-scale adoption. The number of pilots launched, their success rates, and their integration into the company's operations provide a clear indication of how effectively an organization is embracing and executing innovation.

Common Open Innovation Pitfalls: Relying Solely on Financial Metrics Too Early

One major mistake is expecting immediate financial returns from innovation. Relying too heavily on ROI as an early success measure can lead to premature shutdowns of promising projects. This is why multinational corporations use the number of pilots as their main KPI.

Solutions:

- Implement staged success metrics that evolve over time, for example, Discovery (e.g., the number of pilots), Validation (e.g., the success rate of pilots), and Scaling (e.g., adoption rate across the organization, or the impact on revenue) stages, each with its own unique KPIs.
- Measure time to value rather than immediate revenue impact. Here, you should track how long successful innovations take to move from ideation to real-world application and value.

As a common industry standard, many organizations see only thirty percent of their pilots mature into active products or processes. Having said that, I have seen a much higher success rate in my work with organizations, as a result of using the correct methodology. For Menora Mivtachim, for example, a leading insurer in Israel, the successful implementation rate exceeds 60 percent, significantly surpassing industry standards. This rate is the result of several factors, including a strong buy-in from senior and mid-level managers, who are critical in championing and driving adoption.

Interestingly, in most cases where pilots fail to scale, the issue is not with the start-up or the technology itself but instead with the level of commitment and alignment within the internal business unit responsible for its implementation. Without early and sustained involvement from key stakeholders, even the most promising innovations can face resistance or be deprioritized. Therefore, organizations seeking to enhance their innovation success rates must actively foster internal support, ensure alignment with strategic goals, and engage decision makers early in the process to maximize adoption.

Many organizations struggle with innovation measurement because they lack structured methodologies, and executives often focus on broad, intangible goals or measure innovation too rigidly, expecting immediate ROI.

Without well-defined success metrics, organizations struggle to assess whether their innovation efforts are delivering real value. Many companies invest significant resources into innovation but fail to track progress effectively, leading to initiatives that drift aimlessly, lack accountability, and ultimately fail to scale.

I have seen this issue with many organizations to whom I have consulted. Many organizations mistakenly assume that traditional business metrics, such as revenue growth or cost savings, can be immediately applied to open innovation. This is a mistake. Unlike standard business operations, innovation involves experimentation, iteration, and learning from failure, and there will definitely be some failures. **Progress is, more often than not, a nonlinear process, and success may take different forms, ranging from increased collaboration to improved and more efficient internal processes, long-term strategic positioning, and**

everything in between. Without a structured measurement approach, organizations will fail to learn from their mistakes, abandon promising innovations too early, or, even worse, continue to invest in projects that are unlikely to have a real potential impact or value.

A structured framework is therefore essential to correctly measure innovation's benefits, including tracking progress over time. This requires a mix of qualitative and quantitative KPIs that provide a holistic view of innovation efforts.

Over the past years, through research and experience, I have developed my proven methodology for measuring innovation. It is an excellent tool for directors, management, and investors, who are all interested in ensuring the organization is doing its best to remain competitive and ready for the future.

To build this structured measurement according to my methodology, organizations should consider:

- Leadership and Governance: Are top executives actively engaged in open innovation? Is there a clear innovation strategy with dedicated leadership? One way to measure this is through structured engagement activities. Organizations should track the frequency of executive involvement in innovation efforts, such as the number of leadership discussions focused on innovation, participation in start-up meetings, attendance at technology conferences, and involvement in training programs. Regular leadership engagement, such as monthly strategy meetings with innovation updates or structured workshops with start-up founders, can be quantifiable indicators of an organization's commitment to open innovation. Additionally, if innovation is a regular agenda item in executive meetings, it signals strategic prioritization rather than a one-time initiative.
- Culture and Employee Engagement: How many employees are involved in innovation projects? Do they feel empowered to contribute new ideas? Beyond direct project involvement, organizations can measure participation in internal innovation communities, such as dedicated innovation WhatsApp groups, Slack

channels, or internal forums where employees exchange ideas and share insights about start-ups and new technologies. The number of employees engaging in these platforms, the frequency of discussions, and the level of idea-sharing provide a tangible measure of how deeply innovation is embedded in the company culture. Tracking the number of suggestions submitted by employees and those later implemented can also serve as strong engagement indicators.

- Process and Execution: How quickly can new ideas progress from concept to pilot? Are processes streamlined for external collaborations? Organizations should establish and measure SLAs for innovation-related processes, tracking the time from initial engagement with a start-up to pilot approval and execution, including legal approvals. Measuring SLA for these processes and improving its results, particularly regarding procurement and compliance reviews, can indicate how attractive the organization is for a specific collaboration, the potential for future pilots (thanks to word of mouth in the ecosystem), and attract more high-quality deal flow.
- Financial Investment: What percentage of the budget is allocated to R&D and external partnerships compared to the industry standard/previous year allocation?
- Outcome-Based Metrics: How many pilots were conducted in the past year? How many resulted in commercialized products, process improvements, or integration? It is also important to assess how many business units adopted the innovation. In many cases, an innovation starts in one division but can scale across various business lines, maximizing its impact. For example, one financial corporation I worked with implemented a specific solution first for underwriting, and later expanded it to the company's subsidiaries and sister companies. The ability to scale a start-up's solution across multiple business units is a critical measure of an organization's innovation maturity, and organizations should encourage cross-unit adoption to ensure they fully capitalize on innovation.

Common Open Innovation Pitfalls: Lack of a Clear Innovation Evaluation Framework

Without a structured framework to assess and prioritize innovation initiatives, companies may invest in projects that lack strategic value or fail to measure the real impact of their innovation efforts.

Solutions:

- Establish an Innovation Scorecard that evaluates potential initiatives based on specific criteria.
- Require innovation teams to develop business impact approval for new initiatives, outlining expected revenue potential, operational efficiency improvements, or other quantifiable benefits.
- Conduct regular portfolio reviews to reassess ongoing projects and discontinue those that no longer align with evolving business priorities.

Organizations should understand that there is no one KPI that can solely tell the tale of innovation, but the set of them combined shows actual progress and results. These KPIs should also be adjusted depending on the organization's maturity level. Early-stage open innovation programs often focus on engagement metrics (e.g., number of partnerships, pilots, workshops, or hackathons), while more advanced organizations should track business impact metrics (e.g., revenue generated from innovation-driven products, efficiency gains, or time-to-market improvements).

Common Open Innovation Pitfalls: Setting Vague or Overly Broad Goals

Many organizations struggle with measuring innovation because their goals are too broad, such as simply "becoming more innovative" or "driving digital transformation." Without specific, measurable objectives, executives have no clear benchmarks for evaluating progress.

Solutions:

- Define SMART innovation goals (Specific, Measurable, Achievable, Relevant, and Time-bound), such as launching 10 new start-up pilots within the next 12 months.
- Align innovation metrics with business-unit priorities to ensure that innovation efforts contribute directly to company-wide objectives.
- Use tiered metrics that measure both short-term progress and long-term impact.

Among the many metrics available, pilots serve as the most powerful indicator of an organization's commitment to open innovation. The number of pilots reflects the strength of the corporate innovation muscle. A well-structured pilot program allows companies to experiment, validate ideas, and scale successful solutions while minimizing risk. This is also an easy metric to measure and compare over time, as well as with other leading innovators, as it is widely used.

That said, the true test of a pilot lies not in its initiation but in its conversion into integration. Industry studies consistently report an average conversion rate of around 30 percent, meaning that only three out of ten pilots typically scale into real implementation. However, this figure varies greatly across industries. In Industry 4.0, for example, the World Economic Forum had found that approximately 70 percent of pilots fail,[73] while in fields such as AI, the failure rate is even higher, with 88 percent of pilots failing to move beyond experimentation.[74] These numbers highlight just how challenging it is to translate pilots into lasting impact.

[73]N. Chmiko and C. Hutchison, "70% of Industry 4.0 Pilots Fail. A New Center Hopes to Turn That Around," *IndustryWeek*, June 14, 2023.

[74]IDC, "CIO Playbook 2025: It's Time for AI-Nomics," 2025.

Common Open Innovation Pitfalls: Failing to Differentiate Between Incremental and Disruptive Innovation

Although incremental innovation typically yielding quicker and more predictable results, and disruptive innovation requires a more extended timeframe, organizations still often combine different types of innovation under a single measurement system.

Solutions:

- Segment innovation KPIs based on the type of innovation. Measuring such things as efficiency gains, cost reductions, and process improvements for incremental innovation, and new market creation, adoption rates, and revenue potential for disruptive innovation.
- Establish separate evaluation frameworks for different horizons, measuring efficiency and cost savings in the short term, market expansion and customer acquisition in the medium term, and strategic positioning in the long-term horizon.

The conversion rate for my clients is over 60 percent, far higher than the industry average. This, as previously mentioned, stems from the level of engagement, which dramatically increases the chances of scaling a pilot successfully.

Looking at the value chain for pilot implementation, companies should take into consideration how many external collaborations are being tested each year, the conversion rate of pilots into full-scale implementations, how quickly successful pilots lead to new products, services, or operational changes, their cost-effectiveness, as well as how many departments are involved in these pilots. It should be noted that pilots should not be limited to single business units. To truly embed innovation into the company's DNA, pilots must extend across all organizational functions, ensuring that the culture of experimentation and adaptation permeates every part of the company. **Like in many other out-of-the-box processes, the bigger the funnel, the more success stories it will yield.**

Common Open Innovation Pitfalls: Measuring Too Few Aspects of Innovation Success

Some organizations limit their success metrics to a handful of KPIs, without having a holistic view of innovation success. Innovation impacts multiple areas, including culture, customer experience, economic success, technology adoption, and more. Therefore, innovation should be measured holistically.

Solutions:

- Develop or adopt comprehensive innovation scorecards that track process, engagement, adoption, and market impact metrics.
- Use internal and external benchmarking to compare innovation effectiveness against industry peers.

In the appendixes, you will find a questionnaire I have developed, along with KPIs to help your organization measure innovation effectively. Answering these questions will help guide you as you take your next steps in open innovation and its measurements.

Finally, for innovation measurement to be truly effective, it must become part of the company's DNA. This means:

- Aligning KPIs with Business Goals: Innovation should not be measured in isolation but tied to broader strategic objectives.
- Making Data-Driven Decisions: Regularly reviewing innovation metrics helps refine strategies and allocate resources more effectively.
- Balancing Short-Term and Long-Term Impact: While some innovations yield immediate results, others require years to pay off. Organizations must track both with a combination of balance and patience.
- Encouraging a Learning Mindset: Even failed pilots provide valuable insights. Companies should document lessons learned and use them to improve future initiatives.

Open innovation presents many opportunities, but to capture its full potential, organizations must move beyond gut feeling and anecdotal success stories and establish clear measurement frameworks that guide decision making and demonstrate ROI. It should be noted that during the first two years, the key KPI is the number of pilots conducted.

By embedding these best practices, organizations can ensure that open innovation is not just a buzzword but a structured, repeatable, and measurable approach that drives sustained business growth for years to come.

CHAPTER 25

Balancing Short-Term Wins with Long-Term Goals

You can't grow long-term if you can't eat short-term.

—Jack Welch

The challenge of measuring innovation is twofold. Companies must first not only define what success looks like but must then balance short-term wins with long-term growth, ensuring that open innovation becomes not a series of disconnected experiments but a sustained driver of competitive advantage.[75]

Building on the previous chapter, in which I explored KPIs that help organizations assess the impact of their open innovation efforts, I will now outline how organizations can strike the right balance between immediate business impact and sustainable innovation.

Innovation is often perceived as a long-term endeavor, requiring patience, investment, and a willingness to experiment with uncertain outcomes. In truth, while much of that is true, companies cannot afford to wait years to see returns on their innovation efforts. Stakeholders, whether they are executives, board members, or investors, demand tangible, short-term results that demonstrate progress and validate ongoing investments. At the same time, focusing solely on quick wins can lead to shortsighted decision making, where companies prioritize immediate impact over sustainable growth and long-term competitiveness.

Striking the right balance between short-term wins and long-term goals is therefore crucial and serves as one of the biggest challenges in

[75]M. de Jong, M. Banholzer, R. Doherty, & L. LaBerge, "How Top Performers Use Innovation to Grow Within and Beyond the Core," *McKinsey Quarterly*, February, 2025.

corporate open innovation. Companies that successfully navigate this balance, position themselves as both agile and visionary, capable of responding to immediate business needs while still steadily building the capabilities required for future industry leadership.

Many organizations face internal conflicts between short-term business pressures and long-term innovation priorities. This is particularly true in publicly traded companies, where quarterly earnings reports drive decision making, often discouraging investment in projects with delayed or uncertain returns. Similarly, in highly regulated industries such as finance, strict compliance requirements can make it difficult to experiment with disruptive innovations that may or may not take years to mature.

Other common challenges include:

- Unrealistic Expectations: Executives may expect innovation to deliver rapid financial returns, causing promising initiatives to be abandoned prematurely, before they return their investment and generate value.
- Lack of Clear Roadmaps: Companies without structured innovation frameworks struggle to align short-term projects with long-term vision.
- Impact at Scale: Corporate leaders expect innovative initiatives to deliver a substantial impact on the bottom line, while initiatives vary in impact, and the cumulative outcome is, in most cases, providing this expected result.
- Short-Term Market Pressures: Rapid changes in market trends and consumer demands can force companies to shift focus away from long-term innovation in favor of immediate tactical adjustments.
- Speed Versus Quality Trade-Offs: The pressure to deliver quick results may lead to rushed implementations that compromise the depth and sustainability of innovation.

If companies fail to manage these challenges, they risk becoming too risk-averse and therefore missing out on transformative opportunities or chasing too many short-term trends without building sustainable competitive advantages that can later reward them.

The responsibility for maintaining this balance and resolving tensions between short-term imperatives and long-term vision falls on the board of directors. A board that prioritizes only quarterly or annual profit-and-loss metrics risks stifling innovation and its implementation, while undermining the company's long-term strategy.

The most effective way to balance short-term wins and long-term goals is by adopting a two-speed innovation strategy, which involves maintaining some stable core elements with slow innovation and others with rapid innovation. Here, core elements are characterized by a long-term perspective and planned change, whereas noncore elements undergo faster, short-term innovation, characterized by adaptability.[76] This model, used by leading corporations, divides innovation efforts into two parallel tracks:

1. Fast-Impact Innovation (Short-Term Wins): This part focuses on incremental improvements that deliver immediate value, including process optimizations, cost reductions, and small-scale digital transformations. This is measured by KPIs such as operational efficiency, revenue growth from new initiatives, and customer satisfaction improvements. It typically involves low-risk pilots that can be implemented quickly with minimal disruption while providing the organization with quick wins.
2. Strategic Innovation (Long-Term Vision): This part involves transformational projects that may take years to yield results, as well as investments in deep technology, new business models, and disruptive market shifts. It is measured by indicators such as patents filed, strategic partnerships, and industry positioning and requires dedicated funding, leadership support, and tolerance for failure.

Companies that master this dual-track approach ensure that short-term innovation supports long-term strategic objectives rather than distracts from them.

---

[76]B. Bygstad and E. Øvrelid, "Managing Two-Speed Innovation for Digital Transformation," *Procedia Computer Science* 181 (2021): 119–126.

To successfully navigate this balance, organizations must take a structured approach that integrates immediate impact and future growth into their innovation strategy.

One of the most established frameworks for doing so is the Three Horizons Model, developed by Bill Sharpe, which illustrates how current activities, emerging opportunities, and long-term transformational efforts must coexist and evolve.

Below are five methods that leading corporations use to achieve the right balance:

1. Define a Clear Innovation Pipeline, with three distinct categories[77]:
   Horizon 1—The Current Way of Doing Things: How the company currently works, as well as core business improvements (3 to 12 months impact).
   Horizon 2—Transition and Emerging Opportunities: Adjacent opportunities that expand market reach or generate additional value in the medium term (one to three years).
   Horizon 3—The Future System: Transformational innovations that shape the future, including new ways of working, new business models, and new ways to fit the future (three years and beyond).
   This portfolio, or horizons approach, ensures steady progress while maintaining long-term vision.
2. Link Short-Term Wins to Long-Term Goals:
   Successful organizations align fast-impact initiatives with long-term strategic priorities. For example, an insurer can launch a chatbot for customer service (short-term) and later use the data collected to build a predictive AI-driven financial assistant (long-term).
3. Use Pilots to Bridge the Gap:
   Short-term innovation can serve as a testing ground for long-term investments. Pilots reduce risk, accelerate learning, and provide tangible proof of concept before committing to large-scale transformations. This is the most effective way to do so.

[77]B. Sharpe, "Three Horizons and Working with Change," *APF Compass*, January, 2014, 6-8.

4. Foster a Culture That Rewards Both Quick Wins and Strategic Investments:
   Leadership must set the tone by recognizing and rewarding both immediate impact and long-term efforts. Employee incentives should balance short-term performance goals with contributions to long-term innovation projects.
5. Secure Dedicated Resources for Long-Term Innovation:
   Many companies overallocate resources to immediate needs, leaving long-term projects underfunded. Successful innovators secure funding for long-term R&D, ensuring that strategic projects continue even when short-term pressures arise.

A good example of this is Amazon's continued investment in AWS cloud services, which was launched in 2002 and only became profitable for the first time in 2015, eventually becoming a dominant revenue driver for the company.

Balancing short-term wins and long-term innovation is not a simple challenge, but it is a strategic imperative. **Companies that focus too much on immediate gains risk stagnation and irrelevancy in the future. At the same time, those who prioritize only the long term may struggle to sustain themselves in the present.**

Organizations can build a resilient innovation engine that delivers immediate impact and sustainable growth by implementing a structured innovation framework, linking quick wins to strategic goals, and ensuring proper incentives.

This balanced approach enables companies to adapt to rapid changes while investing in the future, ensuring they simultaneously survive and prepare for the future.

PART 3

The Future

CHAPTER 26

Lessons from the Startup Nation's Innovation Ecosystem

Creativity may be hard to nurture, but it's easy to thwart.

—Adam Grant

Israel, a small nation roughly the size of New Jersey, has defied conventional economic and geopolitical expectations to become a global leader in innovation and entrepreneurship. Despite the country's limited natural resources and its ongoing geopolitical challenges, Israel fostered an unparalleled culture of technological advancement, boasting the second-highest number of start-ups per capita, a thriving venture capital market, and a significant presence of multinational corporations, well-earning the title of the "Startup Nation."

Tel Aviv, Israel's high-tech center, has more start-ups per capita than any city outside of Silicon Valley. The city is home to a vibrant ecosystem of innovators, investors, and multinational corporations that recognize the immense potential of Israeli ingenuity.

Multinational corporations have long recognized Israel's technological prowess, with over 500 multinational corporations engaged in open innovation activities in Israel, as well over 300 R&D centers operated by global companies. These centers account for nearly half of Israel's civilian R&D expenditures. Some of the multinationals include for example, companies such as Microsoft, Intel, Google, IBM, Volkswagen, eBay, NVIDIA, and Meta that have innovation centers or operations in Tel Aviv, and many others such as Apple and Merck operate in other parts of the country to leverage Israeli expertise in such fields as AI, cybersecurity, and other areas. Amazon Web Services' commitment in 2023 to investing

$7.2 billion in Israel through 2037, and to expand its operations and build data centers there, further underscores the country's growing significance as a global technology powerhouse.

Lessons Learned from Corporate Giants and Their Start-Up Collaborations: Unilever and Dollar Shave Club

In 2012, Dollar Shave Club entered the razor market, formerly completely dominated by Gillette. It did so by launching its product through an innovative direct-to-consumer subscription model. Instead of competing in retail stores, the company delivered affordable, high-quality razors directly to customers, completely disrupting a business model that had remained unchanged for decades.

By 2016, the company had captured about 5 percent market share. Rather than competing head-on, Unilever acquired the company for $1 billion, allowing it to continue operating independently. The company retained its start-up-like culture, branding, and direct-to-consumer focus, while Unilever leveraged its global reach and supply chain.

Lessons Learned:

1. Corporations should acquire start-ups for more than just product innovation. A new and disruptive business model is equally valuable.
2. Allowing start-ups to retain their independence and branding post-acquisition can preserve agility and customer loyalty.
3. Established companies can use start-up acquisitions to enter new market segments without disrupting their core business.

The roots of Israel's innovation success lie in a unique combination of cultural, economic, and governmental factors, including a deeply interconnected ecosystem, based on a fusion of government support, academic excellence, entrepreneurial spirit, and international collaborations. The synergy between these elements creates a fertile ground for bold ideas and disruption, from which ecosystems, government, start-ups, and corporations can all learn.

One of Israel's most distinctive innovation engines is its military, particularly elite intelligence and cyber units such as Unit 8200, Talpiot, Unit 9900, and Unit 81. These units serve as high-pressure incubators where young recruits develop cutting-edge technological skills, critical thinking abilities, and leadership experience. Many, if not most, of Israel's successful entrepreneurs, including those behind Check Point, Waze, NICE, CyberArk, Wix, and Wiz, emerged from these military programs, either partially or wholly.

Israeli culture is another important aspect, and the famous Israeli "chutzpah," or boldness, directness, and a willingness to challenge authority, has much to do with Israeli success. This manifests in several ways, such as pushing boundaries when pitching to investors, negotiating deals, and solving problems. Unlike in many societies where failure is stigmatized, it is seen as a stepping stone to success in Israel. For that reason, Israeli start-ups are known for their ability to pivot and reinvent themselves based on market feedback.

Israel's universities, particularly Tel Aviv University, the Technion, Weizmann Institute, and Hebrew University, are all deeply integrated into the high-tech and innovation sectors, facilitating technology transfer and commercialization through incubators, tech transfer offices, and start-up accelerators, fueling AI and cybersecurity research, providing innovations in such fields as pharmaceuticals, fintech, and agritech, generating patents and spin-off companies, and boosting innovation through ties between these institutions and industry players.

These activities and talent pool have led to a diverse range of initiatives undertaken by multinational corporations operating in the country. These companies engage in various strategies to integrate Israeli innovation into their global operations, with these corporations typically pursuing an average of 4.4 different innovation activities in Israel. The most common approach, adopted by 71 percent of surveyed corporations, is running proof-of-concept projects with start-ups, allowing corporations to test and refine emerging technologies in real-world scenarios.[78] Beyond these projects, 49 percent of multinational corporations engage in balance sheet investing, directly funding Israeli start-ups or innovation

[78]PwC Israel, "The State of Innovation."

initiatives, while 40 percent participate in corporate venture capital, leveraging dedicated funds to strategically invest in high-potential start-ups. Other activities include establishing R&D centers (37 percent), forming corporate joint ventures (30 percent), collaborating with academic and research institutions (25 percent) and many more.

Thanks to the extraordinary presence and activities of these multinational corporations, Israel's innovation ecosystem has gained unique expertise in understanding how global corporations of different sizes and industries approach open innovation, including which methods succeed and which often end up being a waste of time and money.

Beyond financial investments, MNCs deepen their engagement by sponsoring hackathons, pitch competitions, and similar events, offering coworking spaces and incubator programs, and running accelerator programs to help early-stage start-ups validate their business models. Many of these activities are supported by Israeli government programs, reinforcing the country's standing as an unparalleled hub for corporate innovation.

This diverse and multilayered approach demonstrates how multinational companies leverage Israel's entrepreneurial ecosystem to drive breakthrough technologies and maintain a competitive edge in global markets.

Another factor that supported Israel's ability to position itself as a technology powerhouse was the deliberate and strategic government policies prioritizing research, development, and entrepreneurship.

Some key initiatives and actions by the government that played an essential role in shaping the Israeli innovation ecosystem include:

- The Israel Innovation Authority: Formerly the Office of the Chief Scientist, the governmental organization that provides funding and support for R&D projects, reducing financial risks for start-ups and accelerating the commercialization of academic research.
- The Yozma Program: In 1993, Israel introduced a groundbreaking initiative that jumpstarted Israel's venture capital industry by offering matching funds to foreign investors and insuring investments. This led to a rise in global capital and fueled private-sector growth.

- Tax Incentives and Grants: Israel offers substantial tax benefits for high-tech companies, encouraging both local and international R&D investments.

These policies demonstrate that well-executed government intervention can successfully support and cultivate an innovation-driven economy while attracting significant foreign investment. The first two examples are particularly interesting, as the government took on a substantial share of the risk through direct funding, matching investments, and insurance mechanisms. This assumption of risk was essential to support and encourage innovation in its early stages.

From my personal experience working closely with corporations and start-ups in Israel, I can say that this exposure has given me invaluable insights that I now share with companies around the world: **Israel's innovation ecosystem is not just a success story; it is also a living laboratory that teaches us practical lessons about what really works in open innovation and what tends to fail.**

While Israel's innovation model was uniquely shaped by its geopolitical and economic realities, several of its core principles can be replicated anywhere:

- Government-backed innovation incentives can accelerate R&D and attract investment.
- Strong academic-industry collaboration ensures the continuous flow of cutting-edge research into market applications.
- High-intensity learning environments drive technological excellence. In Israel, this is the military, but it is possible to develop alternative environments to mimic this success.
- A culture that embraces risk-taking and resilience fosters entrepreneurial success.

Beyond these important lessons for governments seeking to expand and improve their entrepreneurial ecosystems, there are also valuable lessons for other stakeholders.

For start-ups and corporations, perhaps the key lesson here is that breakthrough ideas emerge in environments that reward bold thinking, embrace failure as a learning opportunity, and provide structured support for R&D. A mindset of agility and resilience, where experimentation is not just tolerated but actively encouraged, is an essential driver of transformative innovation. Additionally, forging strong partnerships with academic institutions and other key stakeholders, as well as utilizing government-backed programs, can provide businesses with a competitive edge.

For corporations, especially those in traditional industries, adopting a model based on Israel's model of high-intensity learning environments can be a game-changer. For corporations, this means establishing dedicated innovation labs and incubators that allow employees to experiment freely and develop disruptive ideas and solutions. At the same time, they work with ecosystem partners through strategic investments, acquisitions, and various collaborations to bring in fresh entrepreneurial perspectives, talent, and solutions.

CHAPTER 27

Emerging Technologies and New Frontiers

The only way to discover the limits of the possible is to go beyond them into the impossible.

—Arthur C. Clarke

Reaching this part of the book, it should be evident that the pace of change in today's business landscape is unprecedented. Emerging technologies, shifting market dynamics, and new competitive pressures are transforming industries at an increasingly rapid pace.

While what we have seen so far has been nothing short of incredible, the pace is only expected to accelerate, and new technologies and trends will only continue to surprise us and change our world. **The future belongs to those who do not react to disruption but actively work to create new opportunities and stay ahead of the curve.**

Here, I will examine some cutting-edge technologies poised to redefine industries in the near and distant future, including quantum computing, synthetic biology, Web3, and autonomous systems. Understanding these emerging fields is crucial for any company that aims to lead rather than follow.

Emerging technologies are challenging conventional business models and reshaping industries. **To remain competitive, organizations must recognize current trends and technologies and develop strategies to harness their potential effectively, while understanding the forces shaping them, the ecosystems in which they thrive, and the paradigm shifts they bring.** This means that organizations must familiarize themselves with current and prospective disruptive technologies.

Below are several of today's cutting-edge technologies. They are not merely incremental improvements. They represent fundamental shifts in how problems are solved, industries interact, and value is created. Their integration into organizations will define the next generation of business success. Some of these technologies may not be mature then, and others may be replaced by something better, faster, or simply more suitable for the time. What is important is that managers know these technologies, consider how they can impact their business, prepare for their possible maturity and disruption, and most importantly, consider how they can best prepare for next thing, including disruptive technologies and trends that have not yet, at the time this book was written, become mainstream but are poised to reshape the competitive landscape:

1. Quantum Computing: Unlocking Unsolvable Problems
   Quantum computing is poised to revolutionize industries that require massive computational power. From optimizing supply chains and financial models to breaking encryption and accelerating drug discovery, quantum systems will tackle previously unsolvable challenges. Innovators must prepare by collaborating with quantum start-ups and investing in quantum-safe security solutions.
2. Synthetic Biology and Bioengineering: Engineering the Future
   Advancements in genetic engineering and lab-grown biomaterials will redefine medicine, agriculture, and sustainability. Bioprinting organs, designing disease-resistant crops, and using bacteria for industrial applications will become mainstream. Innovators must navigate ethical, regulatory, and commercialization challenges to bring these solutions to market.
3. Web3 and Blockchain: Redefining Trust and Ownership
   Decentralized technologies will transform data security, supply chains, and intellectual property management. Blockchain enables trustless collaboration, automated smart contracts, and transparent research and development funding, thereby reducing reliance on intermediaries. Innovators should explore how Web3 can enhance transparency and efficiency in business ecosystems.
4. Neuromorphic Computing: AI That Thinks Like a Human
   Unlike traditional AI, neuromorphic chips process information in a manner similar to human brains, enabling ultra-efficient machine learning. This breakthrough will redefine robotics, autonomous

systems, and AI in the future, reducing power consumption while increasing adaptability. Innovators should consider integrating neuromorphic technology into AI-driven products and services.

5. Brain–Computer Interfaces: Merging Humans with Technology
   Brain–computer interfaces will allow direct communication between the brain and machines, revolutionizing assistive technology, cognitive enhancement, and human–computer interaction. Start-ups working in neurotechnology will create new markets.
6. Space Commercialization: Expanding Innovation Beyond Earth
   Private companies are pioneering asteroid mining, space-based manufacturing, and global satellite networks. These advancements will unlock new supply chains, improve connectivity, and create novel R&D opportunities. Innovators should assess how space technologies, from materials science, communications, and global logistics, could impact their industries.
7. Advanced Energy Technologies: Powering a Sustainable Future
   Fusion energy, solid-state batteries, and AI-optimized smart grids will transform the way we generate and distribute power. Companies must reassess their energy strategies to remain competitive in a carbon-neutral economy. Innovators should explore how new energy sources can reduce operational costs and enable sustainable industrial processes.
8. 4D Printing and Programmable Materials: Self-Adapting Innovation
   Beyond 3D printing, 4D materials can change shape, self-repair, and adapt to their environment. These technologies will transform construction, health care, and consumer goods, requiring innovators to rethink product design for flexibility and longevity.
9. Autonomous Systems and Robotics: The Next Industrial Revolution
   AI-driven robotics is moving beyond factories, revolutionizing logistics, health care, and service industries. From self-navigating cargo ships to robotic surgeons, automation will enhance productivity and precision. Innovators should focus on human–robot collaboration rather than replacement. More on that below.

10. 5G, 6G, and Hyperconnectivity: Enabling the Future of Communications and AI
    Next-generation networks will provide ultra-low latency, allowing real-time AI applications in smart cities, health care, and autonomous vehicles. The shift from cloud-dependent computing to edge AI will redefine digital infrastructure. Innovators must anticipate how hyperconnectivity will shape customer experiences and operational efficiencies.
11. Biotechnology and Personalized Medicine: Tailoring Treatments to Individuals
    AI-powered drug discovery, gene editing, and digital avatars for medical testing will enhance treatments by making them more precise and effective. Longevity research is also accelerating, promising extended health spans. Innovators must explore partnerships in biotech to stay ahead in this personalized health care revolution.
12. Next-Generation Transportation: Reinventing Mobility
    Hyperloop systems, electric aviation, and AI-optimized logistics will dramatically reduce travel times and costs. Innovators should prepare for a world where autonomous and sustainable mobility solutions redefine global supply chains and urban infrastructure.
13. Ocean Exploration and the Blue Economy: Tapping into Earth's Final Frontier
    Sustainable aquaculture, deep-sea mining, and underwater data centers will open new economic opportunities. Innovators should consider how marine technologies can drive sustainable resource management and climate solutions.
14. Virtual Reality and Augmented Reality: Redefining Interaction and Engagement
    VR and AR are transforming industries beyond entertainment, offering immersive training, remote collaboration, and enhanced customer experiences. In health care, AR can assist surgeons with real-time data overlays, while VR is already revolutionizing education and corporate training by creating interactive simulations. Innovators must explore how spatial computing can enhance engagement, productivity, and experiential marketing across industries.

15. Energy Storage: The Key to a Renewable Future
    As the world shifts toward renewable energy, efficient energy storage solutions are crucial for stabilizing grids and ensuring a reliable power supply. Advances in solid-state batteries, flow batteries, and grid-scale storage are increasing efficiency and reducing dependency on fossil fuels. Innovators must focus on integrating energy storage into smart infrastructure, electric mobility, and sustainable industrial operations to enable a reliable clean energy transition.
16. Carbon Capture and Renewable Energy: A Path to Net-Zero Emissions
    To combat climate change, industries must adopt carbon capture technologies while also expanding renewable energy sources. Innovators already offer solutions to extract CO_2 from the atmosphere, while enhanced carbon storage solutions repurpose emissions into valuable materials. Renewable energy breakthroughs in solar, wind, and hydrogen fuel drive energy independence and sustainability. Innovators must align with policies and market incentives to develop scalable solutions that make carbon neutrality both practical and profitable.
17. IoT and Wearable Technology: A Data-Driven World
    The expansion of IoT is connecting billions of devices, enabling real-time monitoring and automation across industries. Smart factories use IoT sensors for predictive maintenance, while smart cities optimize traffic, energy use, and public services through interconnected networks. Wearable technology, from health-tracking devices to smart textiles, enhances personal wellness, workplace safety, and real-time biometric analytics. Innovators should explore IoT's potential for improving efficiency, personalization, and automation in business operations and consumer experiences. While these technologies are not new, the ability to utilize data and corporations' dependence on it are only growing, particularly due to technologies such as AI.
18. AI and Generative AI: From Tools to Collaborators
    AI has moved beyond automating routine tasks and optimizing processes, and it is now an active participant in decision making, research, and creative problem-solving. Traditional AI models have

already reshaped industries, but the emergence of generative AI marks a new frontier in how businesses leverage intelligence. More on this below.

These technologies are just a glimpse of what lies ahead. Each of these innovations represents a fundamental shift in how businesses operate, how industries evolve, and how humans interact with technology and the world itself.

These technologies require companies to reinvent themselves, rethink current business models and products, and find new ways of delivering value to customers. They also offer opportunities for organizations to overtake current market leaders, as **traditional players who fail to adapt quickly enough will be left behind**.

The future will be shaped not just by adopting emerging technologies but also by how well companies can integrate these innovations into their strategies, partnerships, and business models. Organizations that embrace disruption rather than react to it will lead to the next wave of breakthroughs.

By understanding and investing in these next-generation technologies, companies can futureproof their innovation efforts, attract top-tier talent, and unlock new markets once considered science fiction.

At the same time, **many of these technologies are relevant not just for directly delivering value to customers but also for open innovation itself**. AI, IoT, and quantum computing, for example, are redefining how organizations can identify and integrate new ideas. By leveraging AI-driven market intelligence and technology scouting, businesses can identify emerging trends, assess new solutions, and make informed, data-driven decisions about partnerships.

Beyond scouting, these advancements are also transforming open innovation ecosystems. Virtual Reality, for example, can create immersive collaboration spaces, allowing geographically dispersed teams to work together on real-time innovation projects. Blockchain and Web3 technologies introduce new models for decentralized R&D, enabling start-ups and corporations to codevelop solutions with transparent ownership rights and automated revenue sharing through smart contracts. Meanwhile, sustainable energy solutions, such as advanced energy storage and carbon capture, drive public–private innovation partnerships to address global environmental challenges and solve every-day needs.

Companies that embed these technologies into their businesses, with the right open innovation strategies, will enhance their internal capabilities and be better prepared for the future. They will also attract the brightest minds and most disruptive start-ups as collaborators, ensuring long-term competitive advantage.

It should be noted that there is a "catch" in writing about cutting-edge technologies in the pages of a book. While this book is intended to last and serve as a manual for achieving open innovation success, technologies are evolving faster than print can keep up. While I try to point out the most innovative and futuristic technologies that exist today, it is more likely that a newer, yet unknown capability will present itself soon, perhaps even a day after this book goes to print. With that said, instead of focusing on the specific technologies, organizations must focus on what is common to all of them, which is their immense impact, and why open innovation is the best way to prepare for the next big thing.

CHAPTER 28

The Era of AI and Generative AI

AI will not replace humans, but those who use AI will replace those who don't.

—Ginni Rometty

Having presented some disruptive technologies and trends, it is time to spotlight a technology that isn't just set to change our world in the future but is already redefining our present. Moreover, this technology is a clear example of why internal R&D departments struggle to keep pace due to the rapid pace of technological advancements.

Artificial intelligence has already emerged as one of the most transformative forces in the modern era, redefining industries, reshaping economies, and revolutionizing how organizations and individuals work and behave.

AI-powered solutions are not just enhancing efficiency; instead, they unlock entirely new capabilities, from real-time data analysis to predictive decision making and autonomous systems. Within this broad AI landscape, generative AI (GenAI) is particularly disruptive, ushering in a new wave of creativity, automation, and problem-solving capabilities that were previously unimaginable.

Leaders must understand that AI is not just another technological advancement. In my workshops and lectures, business leaders are often amazed to realize what AI can do for them, with concrete examples. When connected with the right tools, AI's power is tremendous, and the potential is unlimited. We are at the fast evolving beginning of the fourth industrial revolution, which will likely be as significant as the steam, electricity, and computing revolutions. In the future, it is likely to be impossible to explain to people how it was before AI, and it would be as hard to imagine living without it, similar to how it would feel now to live without smartphones.

Lessons Learned from Corporate Giants and Their Start-Up Collaborations: Microsoft and OpenAI

Microsoft has had the strategic and decision-making capabilities to recognize early on AI's potential. Instead of building its own AI models from scratch, in 2019, Microsoft invested $1 billion in OpenAI, followed by an additional investment, rumored to be $10 billion in 2023.

The partnership has enabled Microsoft to accelerate its AI integration, leveraging OpenAI's models across its ecosystem and leapfrogging ahead of competitors such as Google and Meta in the race to integrate AI into enterprise software and web applications.

Lessons Learned:

1. Not all partnerships require acquisition, and long-term strategic investment can be just as powerful.
2. Integrating start-up technology into existing products accelerates mass adoption. By embedding OpenAI's models into its software ecosystem, Microsoft ensured AI became widely used almost overnight.
3. Start-ups benefit from corporate infrastructure, and OpenAI gained access to Microsoft's cloud computing power, significantly enhancing its ability to train and deploy large-scale AI models.

AI is by all means nothing new and has been around for decades, powering applications and tools such as Waze, Siri, Alexa, Google Translate, Google Photos, and so on, all great examples of AI that have been with us for years.

So, what is new?

Generative AI, a subset of AI technology, is a recent breakthrough that makes this era fundamentally different. Unlike traditional AI, which focuses on analysis and prediction, GenAI can generate entirely new content, whether text, images, software code, or even innovative product designs. This fundamental shift expands AI's role from assisting in decision making to actively making them, thus creating outputs similar to human-generated content of various types.

Generative AI, powered by advanced machine learning models such as deep neural networks and transformers, enables organizations to create an endless array of new content, designs, and solutions based on previously learned patterns. It goes beyond simply drawing a logo or creating a jingle for a small business; it can be used to design new pharmaceuticals and optimize complex engineering problems. This technology fundamentally changes how knowledge and ideas are created, offering endless opportunities for those who successfully utilize this tool.

Tools like OpenAI's GPT models, Google's Gemini, and various open-source AI frameworks have made these technologies more accessible than ever, allowing businesses, researchers, and individuals to leverage AI-driven creativity in ways that were once the domain of human expertise alone—and they're becoming increasingly popular.

Although it is a relatively recent development, GenAI has already demonstrated its economic potential. For example, it is expected to impact 16 business functions and over 2,100 work activities across 850 occupations.[79] However, the real competitive advantage will go to those who can effectively integrate GenAI into their workflows and decision-making processes.

It is crucial to differentiate between two levels of AI adoption: GenAI tools, such as different copilots, for employees, versus start-up-driven AI solutions that transform business models. While these tools enhance productivity by helping employees to automate various tasks, they barely scratch the surface of AI-driven transformation. **The true game-changer lies in leveraging cutting-edge AI solutions developed by start-ups and third parties through open innovation.**

While the integration of generative AI tools in day-to-day work is valuable and even praiseworthy, helping employees become more efficient, engaged, and open to new technologies, this should not be

[79]V. Atluri, P. Dahlström, B. Gaffey, et al., "Beyond the Hype: Capturing the Potential of AI and Gen AI in Tech, Media, and Telecom," *McKinsey & Company*, February 22, 2024.

confused with innovation. **Tools like ChatGPT improve productivity; open innovation and start-ups drive transformation.** It's the difference between giving customer service representatives access to ChatGPT to handle inquiries more quickly versus replacing the call center entirely with an AI-driven solution. One enhances; the other disrupts. Both are important, but they play fundamentally different roles in a company's innovation journey.

Consider a bank using GenAI to improve reporting efficiency. While that is beneficial, it is hardly the full potential of this technology for the banking industry. The same bank can also collaborate with AI start-ups to implement real-time fraud detection, hyperpersonalized financial advisory, AI-driven investment strategies, improved customer experience through avatars, and many other options, creating a true competitive advantage. Similarly, a call center using GenAI might shorten customer service response times. Still, a call center that fully integrates this technology could utilize AI-driven voice agents to automate support entirely, thereby eliminating waiting times and significantly improving the customer experience.

Executives must understand that encouraging employees to use GenAI is not just about efficiency but also shifting the company's DNA toward an innovation mindset. Employees who are comfortable with GenAI tools have become more open to adopting transformative technologies from external innovators. This shift is essential, as McKinsey[80] estimates that traditional analytics, machine learning, and deep learning contribute approximately $11–17.7 trillion to the global economy, while new generative AI use cases could add $2.6–4.4 trillion, representing a 15 to 40 percent increase. When applying GenAI to workforce productivity, the incremental impact is even higher, reaching $6.1–7.9 trillion, which translates to a 35 to 70 percent increase in economic potential.

These figures underscore a critical point: **Competitive advantage does not come from small efficiency improvements but from adopting breakthrough technologies capable of reshaping entire industries.**

[80]McKinsey & Company, "Notes from the AI Frontier: Applications and Value of Deep Learning," *McKinsey Global Institute*, 2018.

Furthermore, generative AI is also becoming more powerful every day. Across leading AI labs, such as Anthropic, Google, Meta, Microsoft, and OpenAI, capabilities have advanced dramatically in just two years.[81] Early versions released in 2022–2023 mainly were text-only, displayed limited contextual understanding, struggled with long or complex conversations, and offered little or no multimodal functionality. By 2025, frontier models had become fully multimodal, achieved advanced reasoning capable of multistep problem-solving, demonstrated strong coherence during long interactions, integrated real-time data, and introduced more sophisticated personalization and agentic behaviors.

Beyond that, not only is it becoming more powerful, but its use, and the way humans interact with it, are also transforming. This is particularly true when considering the evolution of the workforce. While GenAI is empowering humans, we are quickly moving toward an era where human and AI collaboration is at the core of new organizational models. The AI Autonomy Levels Framework[82] provides a clear framework for understanding this evolution. Level 1, "User as an operator," is where the user is in full control, and the AI serves as a "copilot" providing on-demand support. In Level 2, "User as a collaborator," the user and AI work together, planning and executing tasks in parallel. Level 3, "User as a consultant," shifts more responsibility to the AI, with the user providing high-level feedback and guidance. Level 4, "User as an approver," is a more passive role where the user only intervenes to resolve blockers or approve consequential actions. Finally, Level 5, "User as an observer," represents a fully autonomous AI that plans and executes tasks without any user involvement.

This gradual shift is likely to result in new organizational structures, particularly the flattening of the organization and thinning of junior roles, as well as the need for supervisors for AI agents who can better work with this technology, as well as employees who will be empowered by AI, and

[81] H. Mayer, L. Yee, M. Chui, and R. Roberts, "Superagency in the Workplace: Empowering People to Unlock AI's Full Potential," *McKinsey & Company*, January, 2025.

[82] K. J. Feng, D. W. McDonald, and A. X. Zhang, "Levels of Autonomy for AI Agents," 2025.

take on new and combined roles, leading to changes also in ideation and product development. A good example is Wand, whose platform enables organizations to build hybrid workforces made up of both human professionals and AI agents. These agents can be recruited, trained, managed, and even continuously evolve, effectively replacing some employee roles while collaborating with others in a shared workspace. This demonstrates how the future of work will not only require humans to adapt to AI but also to learn how to manage AI colleagues directly.

Despite the excitement surrounding GenAI, its adoption has faced challenges. Recent surveys indicate that 36 percent of companies reported no change in growth due to AI, and only 19 percent of companies have seen revenue growth exceeding 5 percent from their AI initiatives.[83] However, this is not due to the limitations of AI itself but rather to a lack of strategy, training, and cultural readiness within organizations. Despite that, 92 percent of companies plan to increase their AI investments over the next three years, and 82 percent expect revenue growth from GenAI during this period.[84]

Many companies also focus on trends, such as GenAI, and overlook not only other critical technological advancements but also what is common to them all—innovation. The common solution to staying ahead of the technological curve is effectively adopting relevant emerging technologies through open innovation. **Organizations that master this methodology are unlikely to be surprised by the "next cool thing" or disrupted by technology or future competitors.** Open innovation allows organizations to successfully implement AI and other technologies, each according to its maturity and value to the company. Once this methodology is embedded, it guarantees the seamless integration of advanced technologies, including AI, but not limited to it.

Research shows that employees are three times more likely to be already using GenAI today than their leaders expect. With that said, more than 50 percent of employees report not getting the training and support they need. Therefore, leaders must invest in training employees and

[83]Mayer et al. "Superagency in the Workplace."
[84]Ibid.

upskilling them, allowing for better AI adoption, including through access to new AI tools during pilots and different incentives for employees.[85]

Generative AI is also likely to result in the restructuring of processes and workflows into two possible patterns: The factory pattern and the artisan pattern.[86] The first model allows organizations to deploy AI agents that can collaborate and navigate work, from end to end. This is particularly relevant for routine processes. In the second model, GenAI tools are implemented at scale to serve as assistants and copilots, enabling them to aid and enhance human work. This is especially relevant in more complex cases that require human judgment.

For example, start-ups like Wonderful demonstrate the factory model in action: their AI customer-facing agents can seamlessly manage tasks across chat, voice, and e-mail while integrating into complex enterprise systems.

The significance of AI, especially GenAI, extends far beyond automation and efficiency; it is also a catalyst for open innovation, as AI-driven platforms enable innovation on an unprecedented scale, breaking down barriers between organizations and democratizing access to cutting-edge insights. GenAI is likely to result in a skills revolution with new workforce and career development considerations, requiring upskilling and new learning journeys for employees.

At the same time, it is also likely to result in new organizational structures, particularly the flattening of the organization and thinning of junior roles, as well as the need for supervisors for AI agents who can better work with this technology, as well as employees who will be empowered by AI, and take on new and combined roles, leading to changes also in ideation and product development.[87] If leaders do not understand how to use such tools themselves, provide their employees with training, and incentivize them to experiment with new solutions, they are likely to fall behind more innovative competitors.

---

[85]Ibid.

[86]J. Kaplan, M. Gu, and M. Sinha, "Enterprise Technology's Next Chapter: Four Gen AI Shifts That Will Reshape Business Technology," *McKinsey & Company*, December 2, 2024.

[87]Ibid.

Additionally, GenAI has a profound impact on open innovation itself, where one of its most significant contributions is its ability to analyze and synthesize vast amounts of information. An excellent example of this is BridgeWise, a start-up that leverages AI to analyze over 90 percent of the global securities market. The company provides insightful analysis, uncovering hidden opportunities and making information accessible, replacing the need for entire departments of investment analysts.

Traditional research and development cycles, which often took years or even decades, can now be accelerated through AI-driven analytics and predictive modeling. By processing scientific literature, patents, market trends, and user feedback in real time, AI-powered systems can generate insights that would take human researchers exponentially longer to uncover. This enables organizations to iterate more rapidly, reducing the risk and cost of experimentation.

Not only is research transformed, but product development is equally disrupted. Earlier in the book, I mentioned Base44, a one-person start-up acquired by Wix just months after its founding. Base44's platform can turn ideas into fully functioning applications within minutes, showcasing how AI dramatically increases efficiency in product development and shortens cycles that once took months or years.

Generative AI takes this further by offering tangible, creative solutions in real time. Whether designing new materials, generating code for software development, or simulating innovative business strategies, generative AI significantly enhances the ideation and prototyping phases of innovation. Companies like NVIDIA, Microsoft, and IBM have leveraged generative AI to create novel products, optimize industrial processes, and even codevelop solutions with external partners in open innovation ecosystems.

Moreover, AI-driven platforms and ecosystems have facilitated the rise of collaborative innovation hubs. These platforms, such as Kaggle, GitHub with GitHub Copilot, and OpenAI's research collaborations and data partnerships, enable experts from various domains to contribute their knowledge and collectively cocreate solutions. Such collaborations enhance creativity and foster a culture where intellectual capital is shared rather than hoarded, resulting in mutually beneficial value for all.

Finally, GenAI is transforming not only innovation but also strategic decision making, fundamentally reshaping how organizations analyze, plan, and adapt to their environment. Just as it accelerates open innovation by synthesizing vast datasets, AI is now redefining the strategy development process. It enables leaders to process complex market dynamics in real time, identify emerging trends, and pressure-test strategic assumptions with unprecedented speed and accuracy. AI-driven tools, particularly generative AI tools, can map competitive landscapes, uncover hidden opportunities, and generate adaptive insights. While human judgment remains central to defining long-term vision, AI augments decision making in several ways, broadening the range of possibilities, enabling more agile responses to change, and facilitating better, faster, and improved decision making. In this regard, **GenAI is not just a tool but a partner in shaping the future of business.**

While AI presents immense opportunities, it also raises critical ethical and operational challenges. Bias in AI models, intellectual property concerns, and security risks are just a few issues that must be addressed to ensure responsible adoption of this technology. Organizations must develop transparent AI governance frameworks that promote fairness, accountability, and compliance with evolving regulations.

AI and Generative AI are not just tools; they are becoming the foundation of modern open innovation strategies. **By integrating disruptive technologies, such as AI and Generative AI, and fully leveraging their potential benefits, companies can become more efficient, profitable, and innovative.**

When integrating these solutions, you should ask yourself: Are we merely making some tasks easier or slightly more efficient, or are we preparing our organization for the future?

CHAPTER 29

The Future of Open Innovation

I've learned that mistakes can often be as good a teacher as success.

—Jack Welch

As our technological landscape and world evolve, so does open innovation. Companies have been shifting from traditional models of innovation to a more collaborative approach for years now, and aided by technology-driven approaches, **there is no going back; only forward**, at an increasingly rapid pace.

Emerging trends suggest that corporations are not only integrating external ideas but also reconfiguring their internal processes to optimize the value of partnerships with start-ups, academia, and other stakeholders.

The sheer volume of emerging start-ups and technologies makes it impossible for companies to innovate independently, and difficult to track innovation manually. To solve this challenge, solutions such as AI-powered innovation scouting platforms are becoming increasingly popular tools for identifying and evaluating potential partners. AI algorithms can analyze start-up databases, patent filings, research publications, and investment trends to predict which technologies are likely to have the greatest impact.

Innovation management platforms that facilitate open innovation processes, such as collaboration and knowledge exchange, are gaining popularity. Existing innovation platforms are now leveraging AI to map global innovation trends, enabling corporations to engage with relevant start-ups more quickly than ever. This trend is reshaping corporate–start-up collaboration, making it more data-driven and reducing the guesswork in finding the right partners.

Similarly, corporate accelerators have been a popular mechanism for engaging with start-ups; however, many organizations are now moving beyond these structured programs. Instead of running fixed-term accelerators, companies are adopting on-demand start-up engagement models, enabling them to work with start-ups in a more flexible and needs-based manner.

Venture clienting, where corporations become early customers of start-ups instead of taking equity stakes, is also gaining traction. Companies such as BMW, through its Startup Garage, and Telefónica, with Wayra, are using this model to integrate start-up solutions into their supply chains while minimizing investment risks.

Open innovation is also expanding into new industries and gaining popularity. While it was initially common only in pioneering sectors, it is now gaining popularity across the board, expanding from high-tech and R&D-intensive sectors to include low-tech industries that are opening up to integrate external ideas, as well as transitioning from large corporations to small- and medium-sized organizations.[88]

We can also detect a shift from partnerships focused on cost savings to those focused on creating interorganizational relationships that enhance value creation.[89]

Another issue that is becoming increasingly important is sustainability and social impact, and we are seeing more organizations incorporate these into their open innovation strategies. Corporations are increasingly partnering with start-ups and NGOs to tackle issues such as climate change, circular economy initiatives, and sustainable supply chains, as exemplified by Unilever's Climate & Nature Fund and IKEA's GreenTech Ventures, and their investments in sustainable innovation.

Generative AI, as previously mentioned, is reshaping how companies approach open innovation itself, allowing them to automate ideation processes and generate new product concepts based on market trends. This enables companies to simulate innovation scenarios, test multiple solutions before committing resources, and enhance R&D productivity.

---

[88]O. Gassmann, E. Enkel, and H. Chesbrough, "The Future of Open Innovation," *R&D Management* 40, no. 3 (2010): 213–221.
[89]Ibid

There are many other ways to enhance cycles, especially as AI technologies continue to mature.

A significant development shaping the future of open innovation is the rise of "sovereign cloud" initiatives. As data sovereignty, regulatory compliance, and digital independence become national priorities, countries and regions are building cloud infrastructures that ensure data stay within local jurisdictions. These sovereign cloud ecosystems are creating entirely new environments for collaboration.

Gaia-X, the collaborative European initiative launched by Germany and France, exemplifies how sovereign cloud infrastructure enables open innovation at scale.[90] Rather than a proprietary cloud service, Gaia-X creates a federated data infrastructure comprising over 180 participating data spaces across various sectors, including health care, automotive, and energy. The initiative brings together large corporations, SMEs, research institutions, and public bodies within a standardized, interoperable framework. For corporations, sovereign clouds can fundamentally reshape how they engage in open innovation by providing secure, regulatory-compliant environments for sharing sensitive data with start-ups, research institutions, and public-sector partners, while reducing barriers to collaboration and enabling joint innovation projects that were previously perceived as too risky due to data governance constraints. In many ways, sovereign clouds are becoming the next layer of infrastructure for open innovation, fostering trust, accessibility, and cross-border cooperation while allowing countries to maintain technological autonomy.

Open innovation ecosystems are continually expanding, encompassing geographical diversification and the addition of new players who continue to join the ecosystem. This trend is expected to continue in the years to come. Therefore, the future of open innovation appears to be more extensive and collaborative, involving an increasing number of participants than ever before.

However, alongside the use of technological tools to advance open innovation, it is essential to remember that its success ultimately

[90]F. Musiani, "Gaia-X: The Bid for a Sovereign European Cloud," *Polytechnique Insights*, June 18, 2025.

depends on people. The commitment and engagement of employees at all levels are critical to building a culture that supports innovation and collaboration. **Technology can enable and scale processes, but it cannot replace the need to inspire, align, and mobilize human beings, because they are where innovation begins and thrives.**

CHAPTER 30

Final Thoughts and the Innovation Imperative

An established company which, in an age demanding innovation, is not able to innovate, is doomed to decline and extinction.

—Professor Peter Drucker

As we reach the end of our Open Innovation journey together, the key takeaway should now be unmistakably clear: innovation is not a luxury, a buzzword, or a departmental checkbox. **Innovation is a necessary foundation upon which modern organizations must build their resilience and relevance.** In a world where the pace of change is exponential, crises unfold in real time, and global competition comes from directions no one anticipated, innovation is the only strategy that ensures survival and growth.

Consider GenAI: No one expected how quickly and significantly it would affect our personal lives and the way we work. In a short time, we have seen a considerable impact across sectors and industries; **this is only the beginning**. Only by working with the ecosystem can your organization remain relevant, learn about emerging technologies as soon as possible, and implement them more quickly than others, while fully leveraging their benefits, rather than merely enjoying partial and limited productivity boosts. This is true, not in 10 years, but now. **Your organization will either innovate or be eliminated, depending on the choices you make today.**

The days of operating in isolation are over. Organizations that continue to cling to closed models, legacy thinking, and hierarchical, risk-averse cultures will not just struggle; they will disappear. I realize that the amount of information in this book may appear overwhelming. There are numerous steps, tools to implement, and obstacles to overcome.

But the result I am hoping for is the opposite of overwhelming; it's hope. The information in this book, compiled through years of experience, is intended to serve as a comprehensive guide for innovators.

My suggestion to you, the reader, is to start with baby steps, set achievable goals, and celebrate your successes, of which I am sure there will be plenty, once you begin this journey on the right foot, utilizing the knowledge transferred through these pages.

The stories shared in this book, from global giants to nimble start-ups, from economic collapses to pandemic pivots, serve as a warning and a blueprint. Blockbuster ignored the signals. Kodak clung to legacy models. On the other hand, companies like Netflix, Procter & Gamble, Ping An, and many others chose to adapt. They did not merely survive; instead, they redefined their industries.

So, as you put down this book, I invite you to reflect on a few final questions: Is your organization prepared for the next disruption? Are you actively seeking external partnerships or passively waiting for innovation to find you? Is your company the one that start-ups want to work with, or the next one they will disrupt? Are you moving fast enough to stay ahead of the curve, or better yet, help define it?

Remember—**time is the only resource you cannot buy**, and the future belongs to those who act now, open up, collaborate boldly, and challenge the status quo. **If you do so with intent, a clear framework, and the courage to lead, you will secure your organization's future and impact how your industry—and perhaps our lives—look in the future.**

The imperative is simple: Innovation versus elimination. The choice is yours.

Bibliography

Angel Capital Association. 2023. "Angel Funders Report 2023." https://angelcapitalassociation.growthzoneapp.com/ap/Form/Fill/LxkeVIxP.

Apaydin, M. 2025. "Optimizing Implementation Schedules for a Successful Post-Merger Integration (PMI): A Behavioral View." *Journal of Business Strategy* 46 (1–2): 11–28.

Arango, T. 2010. "In Retrospect: How the AOL-Time Warner Merger Went So Wrong." *The New York Times*, January 10. https://www.nytimes.com/2010/01/11/business/media/11merger.html.

Arner, D. W., J. Barberis, and R. P. Buckley. 2015. "The Evolution of Fintech: A New Post-Crisis Paradigm." *Georgetown Journal of International Law* 47: 1271.

Atluri, V., P. Dahlström, B. Gaffey, et al. 2024. *Beyond the Hype: Capturing the Potential of AI and Gen AI in Tech, Media, and Telecom*. McKinsey & Company.

Australian Institute of Company Directors. 2019. "Driving Innovation: The Boardroom Gap." https://www.aicd.com.au/content/dam/aicd/pdf/news-media/research/2019/Driving-Innovation-The-Boardroom-Gap.pdf.

Banka, M., N. Chmiel, M. Kostrzewski, et al. 2024. "Understanding Corporate Concerns: Barriers and Challenges in Corporate–Start-Up Collaboration." *Journal of Open Innovation: Technology, Market, and Complexity* 10 (4): 100388.

Bannerjee, S., S. Bielli, and C. Haley. 2016. *Scaling Together: Overcoming Barriers in Corporate-Startup Collaboration*. Nesta.

Beck, R., D. Beimborn, T. Weitzel, and W. König. 2008. "Network Effects as Drivers of Individual Technology Adoption: Analyzing Adoption and Diffusion of Mobile Communication Services." *Information Systems Frontiers* 10: 415–429.

Blanding, M. 2019. "Everyone Knows Innovation Is Essential to Business Success—Except Board Directors." *Harvard Business School Working Knowledge*, January 3. https://www.library.hbs.edu/working-knowledge/everyone-knows-innovation-is-essential-to-business-success-and-mdash-except-board-directors.

Boston Consulting Group. 2023. "Most Innovative Companies 2023: Reaching New Heights in Uncertain Times," May 23, https://www.bcg.com/publications/2023/advantages-through-innovation-in-uncertain-times.

Boston Consulting Group. 2024. "83% of Companies Rank Innovation as a Top-Three Priority, Yet Just 3% Are Ready to Deliver on Those Innovation

Goals," June 4. https://www.bcg.com/press/4june2024-companies-rank-innovation-as-a-top-three-priority.

Brigl, M., S. Cross-Selbeck, N. Dehnert, F. Schmieg, and S. Simon. 2019. *After the Honeymoon Ends: Making Corporate-Startup Relationships Work*. Boston Consulting Group.

Bulearca, M., and D. Tamarjan. 2010. "Augmented Reality: A Sustainable Marketing Tool." *Global Business and Management Research: An International Journal* 2 (2): 237–252.

Bygstad, B., and E. Øvrelid. 2021. "Managing Two-Speed Innovation for Digital Transformation." *Procedia Computer Science* 181: 119–126.

Chesbrough, H. W. 2003. *Open Innovation: The New Imperative for Creating and Profiting from Technology*. Harvard Business School.

Chesbrough, H. 2006. "New Puzzles and New Findings." In *Open Innovation: Researching a New Paradigm*, edited by Henry Chesbrough, Joel West, and Wim Vanhaverbeke. Oxford University Press.

Chesbrough, H. W., and M. M. Appleyard. 2007. "Open Innovation and Strategy." *California Management Review* 50 (1): 57–76.

Chesbrough, H., and M. Bogers. 2014. "Explicating Open Innovation: Clarifying an Emerging Paradigm for Understanding Innovation." In *New Frontiers in Open Innovation*, edited by Henry William Chesbrough, Joel West, and Wim Vanhaverbeke. Oxford University Press.

Chmiko, N., and C. Hutchison. 2023. "70% of Industry 4.0 Pilots Fail." *IndustryWeek*, June 14, https://www.industryweek.com/technology-and-iiot/iiot/article/21267880/70-of-companies-industry-40-projects-fail-a-new-center-hopes-to-turn-that-around.

Davis, C., B. Safran, R. Schaff, and L. Yayboke. 2023. *Building Innovation Ecosystems: Accelerating Tech Hub Growth*. McKinsey & Company.

de Jong, M., M. Banholzer, R. Doherty, and L. LaBerge. 2025. "How Top Performers Use Innovation to Grow Within and Beyond the Core." *McKinsey Quarterly*, February 12. https://www.mckinsey.com.br/capabilities/strategy-and-corporate-finance/our-insights/how-top-performers-use-innovation-to-grow-within-and-beyond-the-core.

Dörner, K., M. Flötotto, T. Henz, and T. Stralin. 2020. *You Can't Buy Love: Reimagining Corporate-Startup Partnerships in the DACH Region*. McKinsey & Company.

Fang, M., L. Cai, K. Park, and M. Su. 2024. "Trust (In) Congruence, Open Innovation, and Circular Economy Performance: Polynomial Regression and Response Surface Analyses." *Journal of Environmental Management* 358: 120930.

Feng, K. J., D. W. McDonald, and A. X. Zhang. 2025. "Levels of Autonomy for AI Agents." https://arxiv.org/abs/2506.12469.

Fusion VC. 2025. "The 2024 Pre-Seed Investment Landscape Report: A Survey of Active VCs and Angels," March 10. https://blog.fusion-vc.com/p/fusion-pre-seed-report-2024.

Gassmann, O., E. Enkel, and H. Chesbrough. 2010. "The Future of Open Innovation." *R&D Management* 40 (3): 213–221.

Gerstner, L. V. 2009. *Who Says Elephants Can't Dance?: Leading a Great Enterprise Through Dramatic Change*. Zondervan.

Giblin, A. 2025. *In-Depth: Age Diversity in Sharper Focus as Boards Examine Composition*. Diligent.

Green, I. 2020. "The Day After the COVID-19." *Innovation Management.* https://innovationmanagement.se/2020/04/14/the-day-after-the-covid-19/.

Hausman, A., and W. J. Johnston. 2014. "The Role of Innovation in Driving the Economy: Lessons from the Global Financial Crisis." *Journal of Business Research* 67 (1): 2720–2726.

Hidalgo, C. A., and R. Hausmann. 2009. "The Building Blocks of Economic Complexity." *Proceedings of the National Academy of Sciences* 106 (26): 10570–10575.

Iansiti, M., and R. Levien. 2004. "Strategy as Ecology." *Harvard Business Review* 82 (3): 68–81.

IDC. 2025. "CIO Playbook 2025: It's Time for AI-Nomics." https://pages.lenovo.com/rs/183-WCT-620/images/CIO%20Playbook%202025%20-%20Its%20Time%20for%20AI-nomics_February%202025_AP242508IB.pdf?version=0.

Kaplan, J., M. Gu, and M. Sinha. 2024. *Enterprise Technology's Next Chapter: Four Gen AI Shifts that will Reshape Business Technology*. McKinsey & Company.

Koporcic, N., D. Sjödin, M. Kohtamäki, and V. Parida. 2025. "Embracing the "fail fast and learn fast" Mindset: Conceptualizing Learning from Failure in Knowledge-Intensive SMEs." *Small Business Economics* 64 (1): 181–202.

Mayer, H., L. Yee, M. Chui, and R. Roberts. 2025. *Superagency in the Workplace: Empowering People to Unlock AI's Full Potential.* McKinsey & Company.

McKinsey & Company. 2018. *Notes from the AI Frontier: Applications and Value of Deep Learning*. McKinsey Global Institute.

McKinsey & Company. 2019. *Place-Based Innovation Ecosystems: Boston–Cambridge Innovation Districts*. Joint Research Centre.

McKinsey & Company. 2024. "The Year 2024: The Year in Charts," December 11. https://www.mckinsey.com/mgi/our-research/mckinsey-global-institute-2024-in-charts.

McKinsey & Company. 2025. "Superagency in the Workplace: Empowering People to Unlock AI's Full Potential." January. https://www.mckinsey.com/~/media/mckinsey/business%20functions/quantumblack/our%20insights/superagency%20in%20the%20workplace%20empowering%20people%20 to%20unlock%20ais%20full%20potential%20at%20work/superagency-in-the-workplace-empowering-people-to-unlock-ais-full-potential-v4.pdf?.

Mehlman, S. 2024. "2024 R&D Trends Forecast: Results from the Innovation Research Interchange's Annual Survey." *Research-Technology Management* 67 (1): 22–33.

Moore, J. F. 1993. "Predators and Prey: A New Ecology of Competition." *Harvard Business Review* 71 (3): 75–86.

Musiani, F. 2025. *Gaia-X: The Bid for a Sovereign European Cloud.* Polytechnique Insights.

Oksanen, K., and A. Hautamäki. 2015. "Sustainable Innovation: A Competitive Advantage for Innovation Ecosystems." *Technology Innovation Management Review* 5 (10).

Ouimet, P. P. 2013. "What Motivates Minority Acquisitions? The Trade-Offs Between a Partial Equity Stake and Complete Integration." *The Review of Financial Studies* 26 (4): 1021–1047.

Paula, F. D. O., and J. F. D. Silva. 2018. "Balancing Internal and External R&D Strategies to Improve Innovation and Financial Performance." *BAR-Brazilian Administration Review* 15 (2): e170129.

PwC. 2024. "AI Jobs Barometer: How AI Is Reshaping Work and Pay." https://elements.visualcapitalist.com/wp-content/uploads/2024/05/1716900017355.pdf?utm_source=The+Shift+Newsletter&utm_campaign=0400791918-INTELIGENCIA_AUMENTADA_2024_11_06&utm_medium=email&utm_term=0_-0400791918-%5BLIST_EMAIL_ID%5D.

PwC & The Conference Board. 2025. "Board Effectiveness: A Survey of the C-Suite." https://www.pwc.com/us/en/services/governance-insights-center/library/assets/pwc-trust-gic-csuite.pdf

PwC Israel. 2019. "The State of Innovation: Operating Model Frameworks, Findings and Resources for Multinationals Innovating in Israel".

Sarrazin, H., and P. Willmott. 2016, July 13. *Adapting Your Board to the Digital Age.* McKinsey & Company.

Schuling, F. 2022. *Partnering with Philips to Innovate for a Healthier World: Holst Centre – 15 Years of Open Innovation.* Philips.

Sharpe, B. 2014. "Three Horizons and Working with Change." *APF Compass.* https://www.triarchypress.net/uploads/1/4/0/0/14002490/sharpe-compass-jan2014-final.pdf.

Smith, B. 2018. "A New IP Strategy for a New Era of Shared Innovation." *Official Microsoft Blog,* April 4. https://blogs.microsoft.com/blog/2018/04/04/a-new-ip-strategy-for-a-new-era-of-shared-innovation/.

Sopra Steria Scale. 2023. "Open Innovation Report 2023," March 30.

Spencer, R. W. 2012. "Open Innovation in the Eighteenth Century." *Research-Technology Management* 55 (4): 39–43.

Spencer Stuart. 2024. "2024 S&P 500 New Director and Diversity Snapshot." https://www.spencerstuart.com/-/media/2024/08/ssbi-director-diversity-snapshot/2024-sp-500-new-director-and-diversity-snapshot.pdf.

Stephany, F., and Ole Teutloff. 2024. "What Is the Price of a Skill? The Value of Complementarity." *Research Policy* 53 (1): 104898.

Trantopoulos, K., M. Woerter, and G. von Krogh. 2024. "Open Innovation During the 2008 Financial Crisis." *Industry and Innovation* 31 (2): 159–182.

Vantage Partners. n.d. "Build, Buy, Invest, Partner: Strategic Options for Growth." https://www.vantagepartners.com/insights/build-buy-invest-partner

Weill, P., T. Apel, S. L. Woerner, and J. S. Banner. 2019. "It Pays to Have a Digitally Savvy Board." *MIT Sloan Management Review* 60 (3): 41–45.

Whitehurst, J. 2015. *The Open Organization: Igniting Passion and Performance.* Harvard Business Press.

Whitehurst, J. 2020. "I Believe My Role Is to Create Context for People to Do Their Best Work." Interview. The Exco Group, August 19. https://excoleadership.com/articles/i-believe-my-role-is-to-create-context-for-people-to-do-their-best-work-%E2%80%8B/.

Zahra, S. A., and S. Nambisan. 2011. "Entrepreneurship in Global Innovation Ecosystems." *AMS Review* 1: 4–17.

Appendix

The Innovation Index Questionnaire

Over more than a decade of research and hands-on experience, I have developed a unique methodology for assessing how effectively organizations foster innovation. This methodology, known as the Innovation Index, evaluates a company's ability to remain competitive, resilient, and future-ready.

The Innovation Index serves as a practical tool for directors, executives, and investors who wish to ensure that innovation is not merely encouraged but strategically embedded within the corporate culture and governance framework.

This questionnaire operationalizes the philosophy by which innovation no longer occurs solely within the confines of one company, by examining both internal and external dimensions of innovation. It provides a holistic diagnostic tool across six domains: Management and Governance, Diversity, Budget and Resource Allocation, Open Innovation, Organizational Structure, and Internal Innovation.

By completing the Innovation Index Questionnaire, organizations can identify their strengths, pinpoint areas for improvement, and benchmark their innovation maturity against that of their industry peers.

It should be noted that this index is not a ranking system but a strategic mirror. By comparing internal results over time, leaders can identify patterns, gaps, and opportunities for improvement.

Used consistently, the Innovation Index enables benchmarking across corporations and sectors, trend analysis over time, strategic alignment between innovation and corporate governance, as well as data-driven decision making in resource allocation and partnership strategies.

Ultimately, the Innovation Index serves as both a diagnostic tool and a roadmap, guiding organizations toward a culture of continuous learning, collaboration, and transformation.

Here are the questions:

Section 1: Management and Governance

1. What is the total number of management team members?
2. What is the number of management team members with a background in technology and/or innovation?
3. Has the board defined an innovation strategy?
4. Is innovation a central mechanism for implementing corporate strategy?
5. What is the total number of board members?
6. What is the number of board members with a background in technology and/or innovation?
7. What role does the board play in driving innovation?
8. Is time regularly allocated in board meetings to discuss innovation?

Section 2: Diversity

9. What is the average age of management team members?
10. What is the average age of board members?
11. What is the gender ratio (male/female) within the management team?
12. What is the gender ratio (male/female) within the board of directors?

Section 3: Budget and Resource Allocation

13. What is the total annual R&D investment budget?
14. What is the total annual innovation budget (in local currency)?
15. What is the percentage of the innovation budget relative to total R&D expenditure?

Section 4: Open Innovation

16. What is the number of new value propositions (product, service, customer-facing, or back-office) implemented in the past 12 months based on start-up technologies?
17. What is the number of pilots conducted with start-ups in the past 12 months?

18. What is the number of start-up technologies integrated into the company in the past 12 months?
19. What is the total financial investment in start-ups in the past 12 months?
20. What is the number of start-up investments in the past 12 months?
21. What innovation-related activities were conducted in the past 12 months (including accelerators, incubators, hackathons, and others)?
22. What is the number of start-ups the organization met with in the past 12 months ?
23. Has an innovation report been presented to shareholders within the last fiscal year?
24. What is the percentage of vice presidents who met with at least one early-stage start-up (pre-Series A) in the last quarter?
25. Does the corporation participate in international innovation initiatives?
26. Does the corporation collaborate with academic institutions on innovation?
27. What is the number of new innovation projects (such as pilots, implementations, hackathons, and others) initiated in the past 12 months?

Section 5: Organizational Structure

28. Does the organization have a designated head of innovation (positioned no more than two levels below vice president)?
29. How are innovation projects managed (e.g., Agile, Scrum, cross-functional teams, or hybrid approaches)?

Section 6: Internal Innovation

30. What is the number of employees involved in innovation-related roles?
31. Do employees have the opportunity to present new ideas?
32. Is there an internal platform or channel for sharing innovation ideas across departments?
33. Is innovation incorporated into employee compensation or performance evaluations?
34. Does the organization track innovation metrics? If yes, please specify.

Applying the Innovation Index

The purpose of this questionnaire extends beyond measurement and numbers. It is a catalyst for dialogue and change. When organizations review their results, the goal is not to assign scores but to uncover the conversations that lead to transformation. The most valuable outcome is often not the number itself but the reflection it provokes among leadership teams: Are we creating the conditions for innovation to thrive?

True innovation flourishes where curiosity meets structure, where ideas are nurtured as systematically as products, and where collaboration transcends departmental and organizational boundaries. This Innovation Index and questionnaire bridge those worlds by transforming innovation from a buzzword into a measurable, manageable, and ultimately scalable practice.

Organizations that use this tool regularly will find that it becomes a compass rather than a checklist, guiding and revealing new opportunities, while ensuring that innovation remains not an act of chance but a way of life.

About the Author

Mr. Itai Green is a global thought leader, strategist, consultant, and speaker on open innovation and corporate innovation. As the Cofounder and CEO of Global Innovation & Strategy Consulting, he advises leading corporations and governments on how to thrive through collaboration, ecosystem engagement, and technology adoption in an age of constant disruption.

Over the past two decades, Mr. Green has worked with hundreds of organizations across various industries, including finance, insurance, energy, tourism, construction technology, retail, and pharmaceuticals, helping them design and implement innovation strategies that deliver measurable results. His approach bridges the gap between corporate structure and start-up agility, empowering executives to turn innovation from a slogan into a sustainable growth engine.

Green is also the founder of Innovate Israel, a leading open innovation platform, and has become one of the most prominent voices in Israel's innovation landscape. A sought-after keynote speaker, he has addressed audiences at major global forums, including events hosted by The Economist, the United Nations World Tourism Organization, the South Summit, and the American Chamber of Commerce. In recent years, he was a featured speaker at AmCham Brazil's CEO Forum, among many other international engagements.

Through his work, writing, and lectures, Mr. Green champions the belief that innovation is not just a buzzword, nor a department, nor merely another corporate objective on the agenda. Instead, it is a mindset, a culture, and above all, a strategic imperative for survival in the modern economy.

To contact the author and book a consultation, a workshop, or any other service, you may reach out via WhatsApp by scanning the following QR code:

You may also contact Mr. Green via LinkedIn by scanning the QR below:

Index

www.ingramcontent.com/pod-product-compliance
Lightning Source LLC
LaVergne TN
LVHW050617100826
845148LV00011B/1626

* 9 7 8 1 6 0 6 4 9 4 9 6 7 *